DREAMS AND DRAMA

Disseminations: Psychoanalysis In Contexts

Series Editor: Anthony Molino

DREAMS AND DRAMA

Psychoanalytic Criticism, Creativity and the Artist

Alan Roland

Wesleyan University Press
Middletown, Connecticut

Published by Wesleyan University Press, Middletown, CT. 06459
www.wesleyan.edu/wespress

First US edition 2003

ISBN   0-8195-6600-4 (cloth)
        0-8195-6601-2 (pbk)
Cataloging-in-publication Data for this book
is available from the Library of Congress

Typeset by BookEns Ltd, Royston, Herts
Printed and bound in Great Britain by Biddles Ltd,
Guildford & King's Lynn

Contents

To Jackie, Tika, and Ari

Introduction

INFLUENCES

For well over thirty years I have had one foot firmly planted in psychoanalysis and the other in the arts. I have been a practicing psychoanalyst in Greenwich Village in New York City, and a training analyst and faculty member of the National Psychological Association for Psychoanalysis (N.P.A.P.).[1] At the same time, I have exhibited etchings, intaglio prints, and watercolors, and have written plays and librettos. It is from this dual background that I have long been involved in exploring the interface between psychoanalysis and art and the artist. This work is a recording of such journeys over a number of years. It is grounded in clinical experience with a variety of artists, in personal experiences as an artist, in working psychoanalytically with dreams and teaching a course on advanced dream-analysis, and in interdisciplinary collaboration with a drama critic and a film critic. Throughout these journeys, I have tried to chart new pathways in thinking about the artist and the artistic process, and about dreams, creativity, and psychoanalytic criticism.

A fundamental premise of this book is to strive for an interdisciplinary integration of psychoanalysis with art and the artist, rather than to tread the road of applied psychoanalysis, which more often than not leads to a reductionistic dead end. From this current work, as well as from my cross-cultural psychoanalytic research in India and Japan (Roland, 1988, 1996), I am well aware of the difficulties of an interdisciplinary endeavor: the seductive sirens of facile integrations and interpretations, and the hidden shoals of profound ignorance of the other discipline or of psychoanalysis. Yet, even with these limitations, I am convinced that an interdisciplinary use of psychoanalysis has appreciably more to offer than the traditional applied psychoanalysis to the arts, as well as to cross-cultural studies.

Psychoanalysis is no longer monolithic in the United States. Sparked by the advent of self psychology in the 1970s,[2] American Freudian psychoanalysis abandoned its exclusive engagement with drive and structural theory and ego psychology. It is now not only involved with self psychology but also with British object relations theory including contemporary Kleinians, various approaches to intersubjectivity, and relational psychoanalysis including Sullivanian interpersonal theory. Individual psychoanalysts are not all pointed in the same direction. Some are oriented toward one particular school of thought, others toward another, still others toward two or three different models, and this can make a huge difference in how they approach art and the artist. It is as important as to what orientation you have as to what you are not. I consider myself a multi-model Freudian analyst; that is, one who is not only knowledgeable about traditional American Freudian models of drive and structural theory and ego psychology, but also about object relations theory, self psychology, intersubjectivity, and the work of Otto Rank. I have never striven for any rigorous theoretical consistency. This is perhaps the artist in me as a psychoanalyst: I can live with inconsistencies and contradictions. This multi-model orientation pervades the thinking in the book.

I also have some familiarity with interpersonal and relational psychoanalysis, as well as with Jungian and Lacanian analysis, but I am not sufficiently trained and grounded in them to use them well. I well recognize that a Jungian orientation, and particularly for the past two to three decades, a Lacanian one, are most relevant for literary and drama criticism. I shall leave this area to the Jungian and Lacanian psychoanalyst/artist.

I have been speaking about psychoanalysts' subjectivity and how it affects their looking at art and the artist, not so much their personal subjectivity but rather the theoretical dimension, what psychoanalytic tradition a particular analyst has incorporated. Still another facet of the subjective identity of analysts that affects their outlook on the arts is the psychoanalytic institute to which they belong. The N.P.A.P., on which I have served on the Faculty and Board of Directors for some thirty-five years, was founded by Theodor Reik in 1948 and is multi-model Freudian in orientation with occasional courses in Lacan and relational psychoanalysis. It is by far the largest institute in the United States to train persons from a wide variety of disciplines, including visual artists, screenplay writers, novelists, musicians, dancers and mimes, as well as professors of literature and film. Its publication, *The Psychoanalytic*

Review, is a major journal of culture and psychoanalysis. Equally important, it has remained apart from the mainstream umbrella psychoanalytic organizations in the United States[3] that have traditionally emphasized either psychiatric training as a prerequisite, or in more recent decades, a doctoral degree in psychology or a social work background. Therefore, organizationally, N.P.A.P. has remained on the margin. This actually makes it easier to work out a psychoanalytic identity and viewpoints on art and the artist that can be significantly different from the dictates of mainstream psychoanalysis.

And then there are those psychoanalytic influences that are usually unacknowledged, those of particular teachers, control analysts, and/or personal analysts. In my own case, I was exposed to three, each mavericks in their own way: Susan Deri, Esther Menaker, and Jule Nydes. Particularly relevant for this book was my long-term involvement with the late Susan Deri in ongoing private weekly seminars for four years.[4] Her broad, innovative views on the basic nature of symbolization was a breath of fresh air in the psychoanalytic field, one that I could easily resonate with as an artist. This was long before her seminal book, *Symbolization and Creativity* (1984), was published. A more personal influence has been Esther Menaker, who enabled my artistic self to flourish and who has always encouraged my following my own bent.

THE CHAPTERS

The book is divided into three parts: "The Artist and the Artistic Process;" "Dreams, Imagery, and Creativity;" and "Psychoanalytic Criticism." Part I consists of two chapters about the artist. Chapter 1, "Psychoanalytic Therapy with the Career Artist," delves into identity issues involved in becoming a serious artist, and major inner struggles that these artists go through in navigating the difficult straits of an artistic career. For being a career artist in contemporary American society requires a degree of initiative, entrepreneurship, networking, and social skills that go well beyond most other career endeavors. This is what much of the psychoanalytic work with career artists is about, not inhibitions in their creativity. This chapter is based on my psychoanalytic work with a wide variety of artists ranging from painters to poets, to dramatists and screenplay writers, to novelists and short-story writers, to theater and dance directors, to filmmakers and video artists and editors, to musicians and sound editors. Four case studies of a painter, filmmaker, poet, and dance director will illustrate my findings.

Chapter 2, "The Artistic Self and Artists' Selfobjects and Transformational Objects: Relational Perspectives on the Artistic Process," is a new formulation of the artistic process related to self psychology and Winnicottian object relations theory. It is relevant to the artistic process in all artists, but is particularly so to those in the performing arts. There is also a new conceptualization of an artistic self that needs particular kinds of selfobjects and transformational objects for its development, functioning, and maintenance. The chapter is particularly oriented toward the artistic process in the performing arts, especially the theater, an area generally ignored in psychoanalytic writings, which so concentrate on creativity in the visual and literary arts. I again draw upon my clinical work with various artists, my own experiences as a painter and librettist, and the work on the artistic process in the theater by Stephen Aaron (1986) on stage fright and Erik Nuetzel (1995, 1999a, 1999b, 2000) on play rehearsals.

Part II is entitled "Dreams, Imagery, and Creativity" and consists of three chapters. The locus of my argument shifts from the clinical situation of working with artists and understanding the artistic self and artistic processes as related to self psychology to the world of dreams, imagery, the primary process, and creativity. An understanding of this world forms the basis for Part III, "Psychoanalytic Criticism." The essential insight for these two sections of the book stems from a dream I had while working on a paper on dreams, now Chapter 3, "The Context and Unique Function of Dreams in Psychoanalytic Therapy." The dream was simply the words, "Dreams are of incipient paradoxes and incomplete metaphors." It took some time to understand the dream but when I did, it called into question the basic underlying assumptions of applied psychoanalysis that the work of art is a daydream or dream dressed in aesthetic clothes; that is, that art has formal elements that give disguised expression to underlying fantasies. In art, however, paradox and poetic metaphors are central to its broader meanings but only exist in incipient and incomplete form in dreams.

This chapter also highlights important factors in working clinically with dreams: ascertaining the relevant context to which a dream is communicating; and delineating the multileveled symbolization of varied facets of the psyche, more so than any other communication in psychoanalytic therapy. The chapter also draws on the updated work on the primary process (Noy, 1969; Deri, 1984) that gives excellent metaphorical expression to varied aspects of the self and developmental stages as well as disguised expression to wishes and unconscious fantasies. It thus goes beyond drive theory and the structural hypothesis toward which dreams are usually related to object relations theory, ego psychology, and self psychology.

Chapter 4, "Imagery and Symbolic Expression in Dreams and Art," draws upon the insights of the previous chapter into paradox and poetic metaphor in art as compared to their incomplete forms in dreams, but spreads its net wider. It delves further into the differences between dreams and art, and relates the standard psychoanalytic view of the primary process, symbolization, and metaphorical thinking as primitive and inferior to the secondary process as based on modernist, Western philosophical assumptions. The chapter then critiques prevailing psychoanalytic theories of creativity in the arts in their varied views of the hierarchical organization of the primary and secondary processes, considering the secondary process in art as only involving aesthetic form. By emphasizing paradox and poetic metaphor as a highly important imaginary part of the secondary process, one that encompasses aesthetic form, a significantly different way of looking at the integration of the primary and secondary process in art and in artistic creativity is presented.

The last chapter in this part, "Imagery and the Self in Artistic Creativity," continues the discussion on artistic creativity by focusing more on the artist's use of imagery. An insight emerged from an etching of mine that within a work of art the same imagery can seamlessly and simultaneously depict powerful unconscious elements within the artist with poetic metaphor and paradox. This is because *imagery bypasses defenses*. These unconscious elements, whether fantasy or body-image or some aspect of the self, emotionally fuel the more abstract metaphor or paradox. This insight is then confirmed and illustrated by a painting done by a recognized artist-patient, and by the formation of a poem by a well-established poet. Artists are rarely changed by their use of imagery even when expressing unconscious aspects of themselves. The unconscious elements are not what the work of art is about, which is unfortunately too often what the psychoanalytic critic surmises, but rather emotionally fuel the artistic vision.

Part III, "Psychoanalytic Criticism," takes off from the insights of the chapters in Part II, from my own work as a dramatist/librettist, and from extensive interdisciplinary collaboration with Gino Rizzo, a noted Dante and Pirandello scholar and critic. We first ran an interdisciplinary seminar together with writers, critics, and psycho-analysts on avant-garde drama, starting with Strindberg and Ibsen, followed by Pirandello, and then by Theater-of-the-Absurd play-wrights. Later, we collaborated on "Psychoanalysis in Search of Pirandello, *Six Characters* and *Henry IV*," Chapter 7. In both the seminar and our paper, we studiously avoided applied psychoanalysis, instead trying to collaborate on an integration of psychoanalysis with traditional drama criticism.

Interdisciplinary collaboration in this or any other field is fraught with difficulties, not the least of which is the narcissistic injury that as expert as you are in your own field, you are a neophyte in the other's. I thought I knew a lot about literature and drama criticism, Gino Rizzo thought he was well versed in psychoanalysis. It turned out we were rank beginners in the other's field. Nevertheless, we were able to work out a collaboration that shed more light on Pirandello's *Six Characters* and *Henry IV* than using either traditional drama criticism or psychoanalysis alone. We approached the plays to elucidate the broader social and psychological meanings of the central metaphors, paradoxes, dramatic structures, and the playwright's anti–naturalistic stance. These were then integrated in *Six Characters* with diverse psychoanalytic viewpoints on splitting and intense emotional themes of repudiation, wounded narcissism, and deprivation that fuel the broader artistic vision of the play of an unrealizable self in twentieth-century society.

Chapter 6, "Toward a Reorientation of Psychoanalytic Literary Criticism," utilizes the framework previously evolved in Part II for a comprehensive survey of the field of psychoanalytic literary criticism with a Freudian orientation. It attempts to deal with its important contributions as well as with its pervasive reductionism. The essay veers away from applied psychoanalysis toward a more interdisciplinary approach that integrates the literary endeavor with the psychoanalytic. Aesthetic form and structure are particularly investigated as to how they have been used and misused by psychoanalytic critics, often related to their assumptions about artistic creativity. The ego psychological approaches of the psychoanalyst and art historian, Ernst Kris, and the literary critic, Norman Holland, are critiqued, as are orientations to creativity and form by Kleinians, self psychologists, and Winnicottians. As mentioned earlier, this chapter does not deal with Lacanian-influenced psychoanalytic criticism, which has predominated in the field over the last two decades.

The final chapter of the book, Chapter 8, is "Pinter's *Homecoming*: Imagoes in Dramatic Action," which deals with Pinter's outstandingly provocative and enigmatic play. By understanding the characters' relationships with each other as both external and internal reenactments, set within the metaphor of the visitor as symbolizing social violence, the play becomes readily comprehensible. The play is a powerful statement on the roots of violence today. Two other of Pinter's plays, *The Lover* and *The Birthday Party* are also explored from these same external–internal dynamics related to the metaphor of the visitor.

READERS

As this book expresses different sides of my own interests and experiences, it should also draw upon various sides of many readers or even particular interests of some. Anyone interested in the artist, creativity, dreams, and psychoanalytic criticism will find the book relevant. While the book deals with some important technical issues in psychoanalysis, it does so in a mainly non-technical way.

Psychoanalytically oriented clinicians should find Chapter 1, "Psychoanalytic Therapy with the Career Artist" particularly relevant if they have any serious artists as patients. Chapter 2, "The Artistic Self and Artists' Selfobjects and Transformational Objects: Relational Perspectives on the Artistic Process," is also pertinent to patients who are involved in the arts. Clinicians would also find Chapter 3 on dreams highly relevant to the use of dreams in psychoanalytic work. This chapter has been used for courses on dream-analysis at various psychoanalytic institutes.

The remaining chapters should be of particular interest to all those who are interested in psychoanalytic theories of creativity and the artistic process, and especially in the integration of psychoanalysis with literary and drama criticism. They also indicate some of the major assumptions of applied psychoanalysis that have resulted in so much of the reductionism in psychoanalytic literary criticism. While some of these chapters were written at an earlier period, they are updated when relevant with more contemporary thinking and contributions.

ACKNOWLEDGEMENTS

I would first like to acknowledge the *International Journal of Psycho-Analysis* and *The Psychoanalytic Review* in which various chapters have appeared in earlier versions. I am very thankful for the stimulating comments over the years of two artist-therapist friends: Stephen Aaron, a theater director and acting teacher who became a psychoanalytic psychologist; and Fred Feirstein, a poet and playwright who is also a psychoanalyst. And of course, my thanks to Gino Rizzo from whom I learned so much about drama criticism, and to Albert Rothenberg, with whom I had long discussions about the cognitive nature of creativity. I am also indebted to the late Donald Barthelme, who did a marvelous editing job on what is now Chapter 8, "Pinter's *Homecoming*: Imagoes in Dramatic Action." I am also grateful for the opportunity to work psychoanalytically with a number of talented artist-patients from a wide variety of fields, from whom I learned a great deal. Then there is Nancy Hagin who has been most helpful in her critiques of my paintings, and Colette Nivelle in a similar way in collaborating on an opera *The New Adam*. And finally, I owe a big debt of gratitude to my family, my wife, Jackie, and children, Tika and Ari, who have tolerated my periodic absorption in my artwork and writing, and with whom I have shared many of my ideas; and to Jackie in particular for allowing a big chunk of computer time, putting aside her own writing temporarily.

NOTES

1. The vast majority of American psychoanalytic institutes require a degree in one of the mental health disciplines. The National Psychological Association for Psychoanalysis is the only psychoanalytic institute to be chartered in New York State to train suitable candidates from any field. Since over a third of its members are from disciplines other than mental health, it is much closer to the composition of the British Psychoanalytic Society.
2. Self psychology is an American formulation by Heinz Kohut that has various points of contact with British object relations theorists, particularly with D. W. Winnicott, but is nevertheless a different approach. Particular analysts such as Bacal

and Newman (1990) in the 1990s tried to bridge the gap by having meetings between American self psychologists and British object relations theorists. By report, communication between the two groups was problematic.

3. The mainstream American psychoanalytic organizations are the American Psychoanalytic Association, the American Academy of Psychoanalysis, Division 39 of Psychoanalysis of the American Psychological Association, and the International Psycho-Analytic Association. N.P.A.P. is a member of the National Association for the Advancement of Psychoanalysis.

4. It has not been unusual in New York City for both candidates in psychoanalytic training and practicing psychoanalysts to be in private seminars with senior analysts.

PART I

The Artist and the Artistic Process

1

Psychoanalytic Therapy with the Career Artist

INTRODUCTION

Psychoanalysis has delved into the psychology of the artist, as distinct from analyzing works of art, along a few major pathways. A considerable literature exists on how artists' psychobiographies impact on their work. Others have analyzed artists' identity, motivation, and relationships to the collectivity and culture of their times. Then, there is a large literature on the creative process, including working with blocks and inhibitions in artistic creativity.

Rarely, however, have psychoanalysts addressed the issue of what it means to be an artist in contemporary American society. First, there is the question of what kinds of conflicts can be engendered in the very working out of an identity of doing serious artistic work, much less becoming a committed artist. These conflicts over to what extent one can or cannot allow oneself to be an artist, and even what kind of artist, usually relate to parental attitudes toward their children's artistic aspirations, which in turn may involve parental conflicts over their own aspirations. Gary Goffman, President of Curtis Institute and a concert pianist, remarked that it is almost impossible to have a classical musical career without full parental support (personal communication).

I have observed socially, for instance, that professional colleagues usually have more tolerant attitudes toward daughters being schooled in the arts than sons, whom they want to have a more secure profession. Being a serious amateur artist is all right as long as the son has a solid career. Daughters are then expected to marry and have children but not to have an artistic career.[1] These attitudes can become deeply internalized into the son's or daughter's self, at times producing considerable conflict if the child is talented and artistically motivated. Or the conflict that a parent with inhibited artistic aspirations can have on an artistically gifted child can also play a major role. And then there are attitudes of one parent toward another, particularly if the other is an artist, that can also have significant effects on the child. All of this will emerge more clearly from the case material.

Second, to be an artist today entails far more than being creative and productive. Psychoanalytic therapy with career artists – painters, writers, filmmakers, dance directors, and others – reveals that inhibitions and blocks in their creative work are usually the very least of their problems and are rarely present or of short duration. Rather it is deep-seated psychological issues in relationships, identity, and self-assertiveness that seriously jeopardize evolving a meaningful and successful artistic career.

To evolve an artistic career in today's American society usually requires a degree of initiative, entrepreneurship, networking, and social skills that is as, or more demanding, than any other career. An inability to network assertively, to find others who are supportive and knowledgeable, to have those who are in tune with one's work where there is often little if any supportive institutional structure, can be the death knell of the career of any creative artist today. In self psychological terms, there is a strong need to have involved alter-ego selfobject relationships as well as supportive mirroring ones; that is, persons with whom one has an artistic kinship as well as others who are deeply receptive to one's work. What is a difficult enough task at best can be greatly aggravated by inner conflicts and self-destructive tendencies derived from internalized early family relationships.

Being an exhibiting artist and a playwright/librettist, myself, I have been referred a number of artists over the years. I shall discuss four cases of career artists, two women and two men, each nationally and internationally recognized, one a painter, another a poet, a third a filmmaker, and a fourth a dance director and producer.

ANGELA

Angela, a Central European immigrant woman painter in her late twenties, came to me because of a failing art career and sadistic love relationships. She had already been married and divorced, in part over her ex-husband being unsupportive of her artistic career. Angela was not at all blocked in her painting. She was in fact quite productive. But she was highly passive in handling her career and despairing of working out a successful one.

Over a very long period of psychoanalytic therapy, three times a week, plus psychoanalytic group therapy, a story gradually emerged that Angela had actually been well on her way to evolving a major career. She had left home and gone to Paris on her own at 16, forming a relationship with a woman mentor who encouraged her to study painting, and then came to New York City for further schooling. Already by her mid-twenties, she was in two major and several minor museum shows; even more important, she had the backing of a powerful mentor who was highly influential in the New York City gallery and museum world, and who had placed her in a major gallery that was actively promoting her career. With the combination of her acknowledged talent, a mentor who was paving the way for her, and an important gallery fashioning her career, Angela was in a position of becoming one of the relatively few highly recognized women artists of today.

Angela, however, at the peak of her early success so infuriated her mentor through unconscious, self-destructive behavior that she not only lost his support but he went out of his way to have her blackballed in the New York City art world. Further, as a result of close association with certain intellectuals who attacked her style of painting, she radically changed styles, completely alienating her gallery. Others with whom she had exhibited in these two museum shows went on to have major careers in terms of both critical recognition and financial success. Angela was often consumed with envy over their success and her own circumstances of struggling hand to mouth and not having a suitable gallery and dealer in New York City. She was only able to support herself by shows in a European city where a woman art dealer fully backed her.

Obviously a great deal went on over a very lengthy analysis, but I only want to focus on major issues that enabled Angela to resume her career after years of struggle, and as a result, to then attain a depth psychological understanding of her earlier self-sabotage. The very first issue involves the analyst's own values around an artistic career. Angela in the beginning could barely afford my minimum fee, and it wasn't at all certain that she could even continue that. She therefore raised the issue of whether she should take a teaching position to be able to continue the analysis, which would then interfere with her painting.

When it became clear that she really wanted to continue full-time painting, I suggested she do so rather than teaching, and we would simply try to work out payments in whatever way possible.[2] She has never been behind.

For a few years, Angela's struggles around extreme passivity and despair over her career, boyfriends (some of them well-known artists) who treated her shabbily, and friends who mainly used her and often gave little support or even denigrated her work, seemed disconnected from shadowy early family relationships. Given what little she said about her family, I wondered how she had ever become an artist. The one matter she repeatedly railed about in sessions was her father pulling her out of school when she was 14 and sending her to work to help support the family. She came from a middle-class family where she was the oldest daughter with five siblings but her father was a compulsive gambler and drinker. Her rage at him was considerable, as it was at other men who treated her sadistically. She left her family when she was 15, feeling she would be used forever by them, and was completely alienated from her father. She worked and saved money in Germany for a year before going to Paris.

A great deal of the relevant psychoanalytic work for several years centered on her differentiating herself from her mother. Her mother was a middle child in a family of nine children, where her own father had deserted the family, leaving them in a destitute state. For a long time, whenever Angela had to make a decision or take an action, she asked herself what her mother would do. Then Angela would do the opposite. It was not so much a case of rebellion as of differentiating herself from the self-destructiveness and deprivation of her mother.

A considerable amount of Angela's envy of other artists was not only generated by her siblings getting what little there was of her mother's attention, but also from Angela identifying unconsciously with her mother's tremendous envy of others, not the least of whom was Angela, herself. This differentiation from her mother's extreme masochism became central in choosing more suitable men to be involved with, eventually marrying a man fully supportive of her artistic career. It also played a major role in choosing others in the art field to be associated with: e.g. choosing intellectuals and artists who are supportive rather than denigrating of painting, which is not infrequently the case today.[3]

There have been two major dynamics that have enabled Angela to progress in her art career. The first has been to seek out people who can guide and support her on major decisions and ways to carry them out in working with dealers, museums, curators, critics, collectors, other major artists, and such. After several years of analysis, Angela formed an important friendship with another woman, who served informally as her agent, and with whom she shared the same aesthetic in art. It was both an alter-ego and idealizing selfobject relationship. This woman, who knew her way around art circles and the monied social circles that are often involved, gave a great deal of advice to Angela, not the least of which was to be far more up front in telling others what she wanted from them. Angela had to learn a totally different way of being in the world with others from how she had been in her family, as the one who always took care of her siblings but could ask little for herself from her overwhelmed, masochistic mother and dysfunctional father. This opened up a great deal of her early family relationships for analytic discussion. From this relationship with her agent, Angela has gone on to seeking others who can give her the kind of advice and expertise on handling a major art career. Angela has been able to internalize much of the advice and use it on her own.

This clarified intermittent transference reactions where she experienced me as a distant figure with whom she couldn't make herself heard or understood, and from whom she felt she didn't get anything. At those times, I was obviously the overwhelmed mother.

Second, on a much more unconscious level, as Angela became somewhat more successful in having more shows and selling more paintings, it suddenly emerged through dreams that Angela had a repressed childhood relationship with her father from ages 7 to 12. He had at that time strongly encouraged her to develop her artistic talent and was very proud of her. She had been his favorite. It was in her teenage years that as her mother became more and more enraged at Angela's father for his gambling and drinking, that all of the children were forbidden to have a relationship with their father. And in fact, when her father died when Angela was in her early twenties, all of the children were forbidden to mourn him by their mother. Angela had deeply internalized her mother's attitudes toward her father.

It was just this experience that was unconsciously repeated with her mentor. From an early supportive relationship, Angela then unconsciously dismissed him by not acknowledging his role as her mentor in an important museum catalogue, which infuriated him. In effect, she had done this earlier in an alliance with her mother. This, too, had to be interpreted in the transference with me, where there was sometimes a tendency to dismiss me. The recovered memory of her childhood relationship with her father clarified a strong idealizing transference where I was filling in for the idealized father of her childhood whom she later had to denigrate and dismiss.

As her feelings from childhood became available around her father, and intense feelings of grief emerged for the first time, her painting suddenly changed. From being known as a daring, talented colorist, she suddenly changed to painting in black and white, often with drips of paint expressing her tears. Her painting became her mourning. Then she spontaneously began blacking out half of her paintings, the blacking out symbolizing how she in an unconscious alliance with her mother had to block out her feelings of grief for her father. One of these paintings is in a major art museum in Europe.

A further development entailed following the advice of her friend and agent that, to be really accepted in Europe as an important painter, it would help enormously for Angela to write about painting for European art magazines. She was at first completely blocked in writing, in considerable contrast to her painting. The only voice Angela had at home was her drawing and painting, which her mother could not decipher. Otherwise, Angela was to have no opinion of her own. Writing symbolized having a verbal voice, and one that might disagree with the accepted critical viewpoints of today that so denigrate painting for conceptual, minimalist, and installation art. Enormous anxiety was attached to writing as it so involved self-assertion of her own viewpoint. As this was analyzed, the transference mainly changed to an alter-ego selfobject relationship. Knowing that I write a great deal, Angela was able to come to session to voice and write thoughts that initially she could not do on her own but has gradually been able to do so. Writing in session continued for some time before she was able to write on her own.

As Angela became more and more recognized both in gallery exhibits and particularly museum shows, another transference dynamic emerged that took a very long time to understand. After each success, she became enraged at one man or another, often her husband or a male member of the psychoanalytic group she is in, occasionally me or a friend, all of whom she experienced as doing her in in some way or another. Her successes aroused intense paranoid anxieties, which she handled by attacking the other. It was only through dreams that we eventually understood that these reactions to success were related to an older brother sadistically attacking her physically when she was around 10 to 12 years old and had gotten considerable attention from her father for her artistic talent. He even made some attempts to kill her, which, years later, he acknowledged, including an attempt on a younger sister. Interestingly enough, I have another career artist whose older brother made two acknowledged, serious attempts to kill her during her childhood when she was her father's favorite. After many years of psychoanalytic therapy, it became clear that Angela's earlier association with intellectuals who so attacked her style of painting was an unconscious repetition of her sadistic older brother. At that time when she was so highly successful in her mid-twenties, it resulted in a drastic change in her painting which then became another nail in the coffin of her career. She had unconsciously retreated from being the object of her brother's envy and hostility.

Currently, she has had a retrospective of her paintings in the United States and Europe, together with a major gallery taking her on in her home country. She has also published several articles about her way of painting in major European art magazines. As a result of the recognition she has received, she is finally reasonably comfortably off financially.

HAL

Hal, an internationally recognized avant-garde filmmaker, came for therapy because of marital discord and constant struggles over how much he should pursue his filmmaking and artistic career. Hal's conflict over how much he could allow himself to be deeply involved in his art and career was closely related to his relationship with his father, and as we realized much later to his mother as well. In the earlier part of the once-a-week psychoanalytic therapy that continued for several years, Hal was quite angry at and alienated from his father, whom he portrayed as being against Hal becoming an artist. His father had apparently had artistic aspirations himself but because of family pressures, he became a lawyer and deeply buried this artistic part of himself. But not entirely.

It later surfaced that his father had been closely involved with a number of famous artists, and played a major role in shaping national legislation that was of enormous financial benefit to a wide variety of artists and artistic companies. Many artists' careers and performing companies were enabled to flourish due to his father's legislative initiatives. At the same time that this was occurring, during Hal's adolescent and early college years, his father was adamantly against Hal becoming an artist of any kind, and in fact withdrew funding Hal's college tuition, which he could well afford, when Hal decided to major in filmmaking. Hal obviously represented a forbidden part of his father, a part that the latter tried to squash in Hal as it apparently had been in himself. Hal, however, had been able to turn to male mentors in college to enable him to develop artistically, one of whom enabled him to get an art scholarship to continue in college. After college, an older woman artist became his lover and further fostered Hal's artistic development.

Yet, another important part of Hal's inner struggle to be an artist was actually a profound identification with his father and his father's conflict. Hal, like many filmmakers in the United States today, is also an academic. During the therapy, as Hal resolved his resentment at his father, and from pressure from his wife to bring in more money, he took an administrative position at his State University of New York college that paid significantly more. He then did a great deal to upgrade the art department, as well as to further the arts at the college, itself. Symbolically, this was quite similar to his father's legislative efforts for artists; but being successful at this like his father took enormous amounts of time and effort, seriously detracting from Hal's involvement in his filmmaking.

But there was even more to his inner conflicts over his artistic career. At first glance, Hal's gravitating to an artistic identity seemed to an appreciable extent to be related to his mother who was a musician, and who had encouraged Hal in his artistic aspirations. However, as therapy progressed, a major family dynamic emerged that has also affected Hal being able to devote sufficient time to his artistic career. As his father became more and more involved in important legislative campaigns to help artists, which entailed frequent trips to Washington, D.C., he and Hal's mother became estranged and eventually divorced. His mother bitterly complained to Hal and his sisters about his father's professional involvements with artists that frequently took him away from the family and significantly interfered with his earning capacities.

This family dynamic seriously affects Hal to the extent he is deeply identified with his father. As Hal strives to live out his identity as a filmmaker, he feels constant pressure that he is deserting his family. He has been very vulnerable to any criticism from his wife for devoting too much time to his creative work and to his career: such as going to various international conferences to show his films, networking for new grants, seeing new works, and meeting new artists as well as resuming contacts with old ones for his international reputation to grow. His vulnerability to his wife's criticism is not only due to his mother's attacks on his father, but also to a lifelong relationship with his mother, a Holocaust survivor. Similar to other children of Holocaust survivors, Hal is very vulnerable to his mother's moods, and therefore his wife's, feeling extreme guilt if he is upsetting either. Conflicts over expressing anger to either are considerable.

An old story was repeatedly told in his Eastern European Jewish family that further symbolizes this conflict. The artistic abilities and sexuality of gypsies are greatly admired but then admonished as being very dangerous to the well-being of the family. Thus, the artist and the responsible family man are experienced in opposition to each other. One can be only one or the other.

By delving into these varied psychodynamics, psychoanalytic therapy has enabled Hal to become much more involved in his artistic work and in his career, including the necessary ingredient of much more networking. He has given up his administrative position to return to teaching, with considerably more time to do his filmmaking. Conflicts over it are still present but in a significantly diminished way.

Parenthetically, Hal being a child of a Holocaust survivor, his mother, has played a major role in his creative work. All of his films are either directly concerned with or indirectly connected to the Holocaust. On this, there is little if any inner conflict.

JOHN

A nationally recognized poet with three well-reviewed books of poetry, John came for twice-a-week psychoanalytic therapy and group therapy for over three years because he had become completely stymied in his career, as well as having difficult problems in his marriage. He was unable to get another book of poetry published, one that he had worked on for a few years. He had for years withdrawn from the poetry social scene, as well as from committees at the New England university where he taught in the English Department while still writing. It became apparent that his inability to network with the movers and shakers in the poetry world of publishing, a shrinking domain, was adversely affecting his ability to publish.

Unlike both Angela and Hal, John's parents had both given him full support and encouragement as a child and teenager to be a poet. And indeed, John had some of his poems published in major literary magazines as a teenager. Both parents were involved in their own art but made a living in a commercial art business.

There were of course many issues addressed in the psychoanalytic therapy, but I shall only stress those most relevant to John's career as a poet. We gradually delved into John's character traits of being highly obsequious, passive, hiding his feelings particularly angry ones, and trying to please and placate others being fearful of their opinion of him. He avoided all social situations as he found them too stressful. We found these traits were primarily defensive maneuvers in growing up in a family where his mother had a serious drinking problem, and was frequently given over to volatile emotional states, including rages. John did everything possible to avoid his mother's outbursts. His father rarely protected John from his mother.

This analysis gradually enabled John to become far more assertive and interactive in the therapy relationship, enabling him to participate much more actively in poetry series and in the social gatherings afterward, as well as on college committees central to his position as an esteemed professor in his department. As John became more socially assertive on the poetry scene and at the university, he decided to establish a new poetry series himself. He published other major mid-career poets who were having difficulties getting published. He thus became a mover and shaker himself in the poetry world. Eventually, through his enhanced contacts he got his fourth book of poetry published, again well reviewed.

There was still another factor that had to be handled for John to become more active and assertive in his career and in relationships with his wife and others. He had been a compulsive although not heavy marijuana smoker for many years, which contributed to his passivity. I referred him to a psychiatrist who diagnosed John as having a mild depression and put him on a very low dose of an anti-depressant. This enabled John to stop using marijuana, and also helped him to be a more actively expressive person.

MARJORIE

Marjorie, a co-director and co-producer of an innovative, modern dance company came to psychoanalytic therapy because she felt she was not functioning well either in her career or personal life. She was in deep mourning over the recent death of her mother with whom she had a highly involved and problematic relationship. Her personal and artistic life was completely intertwined as her co-director and co-producer, Cecile, had been her lover as well as her artistic partner. Other dancers, choreographers, and musicians with whom she closely worked often enough became her friends. There were only a very small handful of friends outside of these circles, one of whom referred her to me.

Important issues quickly surfaced in the therapy that had far-reaching ramifications in her professional life. Marjorie is a highly intelligent, articulate woman who would talk freely in sessions. It struck me, however, that much of what she said I couldn't really understand. Was she talking on a level of metaphors and abstractions that I had trouble apprehending; or was something more problematic taking place? I often asked her to explain herself further when I didn't understand what she was really saying. As we delved into this manner of communication, it emerged that Marjorie was hiding through words. That is, she would say a great deal while her inner thoughts and feelings remained hidden. Being bright, it all sounded highly intelligent.

As we continued to analyze this way of communicating, she has gradually been able to talk more directly. Since Marjorie has to deal with a whole host of people, ranging from artists to theater owners to board members to grants organizations, her being able to express herself more cogently has been of enormous help. Through this analysis, we found it directly related to important family dynamics. Except for a childhood period from around 5 to 8 when she had a close relationship with her father, the latter has been highly critical in a denigrating way of Marjorie for the rest of her life. Moreover, there was also a dynamic of family members ganging up on her: frequently her father and an older sister, and sometimes her father and mother together. She therefore learned to appear sociable and communicative but hid what she really thought and felt so it wouldn't be used against her.

Marjorie had an uphill battle maintaining a sense of self-worth against her father's denigrating criticisms. For years she had invited her parents, who lived in Virginia, to performances of her company. Her father replied that he and her mother would only come to New York City if Marjorie's company had a production on Broadway. And indeed they did come when there was a performance in a Broadway theater that received rave reviews. After the performance was over, her father remarked in his inimitable way that he always knew Marjorie should have gone into another field, like advertising.

This dynamic with the father became played out in the transference when a choreographer, a friend of mine, approached Marjorie to develop one of his works. On the one hand, she was deeply gratified by his telling her how highly he thought of her work as a director-producer; on the other hand, she really didn't feel his piece was what she wanted to direct and produce. Their aesthetic was different. She struggled for well over a year to be able to dissociate herself from directing and producing his work. Behind her struggle to be more up front with him was a hidden transference projection that I would yell and scream at her, similar to her father, for turning down my friend's work. She saw us as teaming up against her. This had gone on for many months until she was finally able to bring it up. All of this occurred after I had assured her from the very beginning that I would have no conversation with my friend over their collaboration together. Marjorie's difficulty to be up front in other artistic relationships was damaging to running the company.

As much as Marjorie's relationship with her denigrating father affected her career, her relationship with her mother had an even more profound effect. Originally, her mother, with her father's acquiescence, encouraged Marjorie as a child and teenager to take dance and music lessons. They were both quite pleased at the considerable talent she showed, and still supported her when she majored in dance in college. It was only when Marjorie on her own went on to graduate school and then a career in dance that her parents became very negative about it.

The more problematic aspects of her relationship with her mother emerged in her long-term relationship with Cecile. Cecile, a woman some years older than Marjorie, was originally a talented dancer, later a choreographer, who then moved into being a director-producer. Cecile could at times be quite masochistic in some of her theatrical relationships. When Cecile and Marjorie had both worked for years developing two major pieces that were put on Broadway, in spite of a contract stating they would get equal billing, they gave in to the producers who publicized the work as being entirely their own. Marjorie, against her better judgment, went along with Cecile's masochism. Time and again, within their own company, Marjorie passively submitted to some of Cecile's poor business decisions and bad judgments over keeping personnel who were functioning poorly. Ironically, one of Marjorie's strengths was in identifying with the practical business side of her difficult father, enabling her to have rather good judgment in many difficult situations.

Her going along with Cecile's masochism, had its roots in Marjorie's relationship with her mother, who came from a large New England Italian family with very close extended family relationships. When they had moved to Virginia when Marjorie was 10 because of the father's corporation transferring him there as a manager, her mother became and remained depressed. Her depression seemed related not only to the loss of the extended family relationships, but to serious problems with her husband. Her mother had picked Marjorie from her three siblings to be her designated caretaker. They had a highly symbiotic relationship in which Marjorie deeply identified with her mother in the latter's masochistic position toward Marjorie's father.

Marjorie's relationship with Cecile was a highly complex one. Artistically, Cecile had originally been a mentor for Marjorie. Over the years they were intense alter-ego selfobjects for each other, discussing endlessly the aesthetics as well as the practicalities of innovative dance theater works they were developing together, both being remarkably on the same wavelength. It was a highly productive artistic relationship.

On the other hand, first in their love relationship and then later as close friends, Marjorie was symbiotically and passively tied to Cecile, taking care of her personally and in the office. Marjorie found it very difficult to assert any kind of an independent existence apart from Cecile, including being able to follow her own initiatives in the office. Moreover, since Cecile had a chronic illness, Marjorie was her perpetual caretaker.

As we explored Marjorie's symbiotic relationship with her mother and how it became reproduced with Cecile, Marjorie began to assert her own independent identity apart from Cecile both in her career and personal life. She gradually took major positions in important arts organizations, having a voice of her own and emerging from always existing in Cecile's shadow. She gradually began to differ openly with Cecile over important business decisions and to ease out personnel who were not functioning well. In her personal life, she developed friends apart from Cecile but shied away from having another lover.

There was still another family dynamic that Marjorie played out transferentially in her artistic relationships that have been self-destructive. Twice she referred talented dancers she had helped to develop to an agent she knew to help them with their careers, while she expected these artists would still retain their loyalty to the dance theater company. But the agent had ambitions of her own to produce and direct, and therefore seduced these artists away from Marjorie and Cecile. Upon delving into this, it turned out that Marjorie was not so unaware of the agent's ambitions. As we probed into this masochistic behavior, we found it related to Marjorie's relationship with an older sister who would be very friendly to Marjorie and then set her up to be sharply criticized by their father, or would do her in some other way.

After over three years of Marjorie's psychoanalytic therapy, Cecile suddenly developed cancer and died within a very short time. It was a devastating blow to Marjorie. It was a most painful loss of someone who was an ongoing important artistic selfobject, as well as their still having a very close emotional friendship. Fortunately, through the psychoanalytic therapy, Marjorie attained much more of an independent identity, and has been able to carry on her dance company in a dynamic way. In fact, she has been able to make a number of positive changes in the personnel and on the Board of Directors, and to put the organization on a more solid financial basis. All of this would have been more difficult if Cecile were still alive.

CONCLUSIONS

The issue of having an artistic identity and working with commitment at one's art can vary considerably from one artist to another. Angela, John, and Marjorie had little conflict over this: it being Angela's only way of being herself in the world, John being fully supported by both parents, and Marjorie being supported by her parents for schooling in the arts through college. Whereas Hal's father seriously interfered with Hal's artistic aspirations and engendered conflict, further exacerbated by certain family dynamics and attitudes.

All four patients experienced severe conflicts and/or inhibitions over developing and handling their artistic careers, with its concomitant social networking and entrepreneurial initiative. These inhibitions and conflicts were related to varied internalized family dynamics, childhood relationships, and inner conflicts of the parents, themselves. Through psychoanalytic therapy, all four have been able to handle their artistic careers far better than before as well as their personal relationships.

None of these four patients ever experienced any significant blocks in their creative work.

NOTES

1. Balancing a family life with an art career presents special problems for women artists. For one writer's experience, see Jane Lazarre's (1978) "The Mother-Artist: Woman as Trickster."
2. Coming from a family where my father was a painter and my grandfather an actor on the Yiddish stage in New York City, I am well attuned to the values and difficulties of having an artistic career.
3. For the last three plus decades, there has been a critical denigration of painting in favor of conceptual art, minimalism, and installation and performance art.

2

The Artistic Self and Artists' Selfobjects and Transformational Objects: Relational Perspectives on the Artistic Process

INTRODUCTION

Artists do not create in a vacuum. Besides having a plethora of internal objects which they draw upon for their work, they are also internally populated by other artists living and dead who play a major role in their art. And in the performing arts – in the theater, music, and dance – they are constantly interrelating and creating with other actors, musicians, and dancers.

In all of the arts there are idealized figures,[1] deceased and living, who serve as important models for the artist to aspire to; or whose work the artist greatly admires. Then, there are other more denigrated figures whose art serves as a model to be studiously avoided. There are also other artists, often mentors, who help the young artist develop, to be a transformational object (Bollas, 1987) to the artist's developing self or who are deeply in tune with the artist's talent and sensibility (Kainer, 1990; Hagman, 2000). The mentor–teacher has a somewhat different ring to it than the usual teacher who enables the student to learn the basic techniques as well as the aesthetics of the field. Learning the basic skills and knowledge of the field is one matter, having someone to help draw out one's vision and particular voice is something else. Then, there are fellow artists who are on the same wavelength, or a similar enough wavelength, to enable young artists to move forward in their artistry. Such alter-ego collaboration often occurs earlier in an artist's development but may also happen much later in an artist's career and can greatly enhance each of the artists' creativity. Witness Picasso and

Braque on their fertile formulation of cubism, and Wordsworth and Coleridge in 1797–98 when they jointly published *Lyrical Ballads*, or of Marjorie and Cecile (see last chapter in this book) in the development of an innovative dance company.[2]

From a self-psychological viewpoint, these idealized figures, attuned mentors, and fellow artists on a similar wavelength are all considered selfobjects; that is, persons who enhance the esteem, cohesiveness, and development of the artist's self. Similarly, from a Winnocottian object relations standpoint, these figures play a transformational role in the development of the artist's self. It is not that the artist seeks such figures for a return to the original transformational object, the mother of infancy who helped facilitate and shape her child's self. Rather, it is the necessity to have these transformational objects to develop another major dimension of the self, an artistic self.

THE ARTISTIC SELF

To speak of the artist's self is too general. We are not all of one piece. Fairbairn's emphasis on different libidinal ties to various figures of childhood influenced relational psychoanalysts[3] such as Benjamin, Messler, and Mitchell to develop the idea of different selves with their own organization and history. There are different selves or at the very least, self states, within all of us. From a cross-cultural perspective, Indian and Japanese women speak of an experiential self that varies far more with their relationships than what they see as the relative consistency of American women (Roland, 1988, 1996).[4] Thus, in everyone the self is complex and varies significantly across radically different cultures.

More to the point than the artist's self is an artistic self that may exist to a certain degree in a fair number of people but is only developed in a relatively few. As I described in the previous chapter, parental attitudes and expectations play a major role in the extent to which an artistically talented child and adolescent can develop an artistic self, as well as identifications and counter-identifications with a parent who is an artist. In Hal, where his father's own conflicts over being an artist seriously interfered with Hal developing an artistic self, Hal had enough encouragement and identification with his musician mother to go on to college and persevere as a film major. He was then able to have mentors and close relationships with other film students, as well as later being involved with an older woman artist, to develop his artistic self.

In an artistic self there is an inborn aesthetic sensibility and resonances as well as talent in one or more fields of art. This not only draws the person to a field(s) of art but perhaps more important, to a particular tradition within that field. For every field of art has a number of traditions. Almost all of a particular artist's selfobjects and transformational objects, whether it be idealized figures, mentors, or fellow artists, are within the particular tradition of the field of art in which an artist is involved. The artist then spends his or her life in a dialogue with the tradition: trying to live up to the best of it while creatively modifying it.[5]

It is also apparent that artists can resonate with artistic traditions far from their own culture or combine traditions that might seem quite disparate. Thus, Angela (see Chapter 1) deeply resonates with modernism in its abstract, non–representational, minimalist aesthetic; but she is also in tune with one of the Asian art traditions where inner realities are expressed metonymically rather than symbolically in painting.[6] She furthermore has a profound resonance with ancient Mediterranean vases that strike a particular cord in her, and which she occasionally uses in her paintings. Their color and multiple shapes and their evidence of an ancient culture carry a certain vibrancy for her. Symbolically, vases are obviously a feminine symbol but the particular symbol chosen has more to do with the sensibility of her artistic self.

When artists have teachers or others who are not attuned to the sensibility of their artistic self, it can be very painful. Angela voiced some of this same pain and inner struggle when major teachers in her graduate art school declared that painting was passé, that conceptual, performance, and installation art is the art of today. This was such a threat to her artistic self that she painted secretly in her studio rather than in class. Fortunately, other idealized faculty such as Mark Rothko stood firmly for painting. In recent years, she has also voiced her vulnerability to comments on new paintings from various artists, curators, or art critics. She has more than once ruined a painting from critiques out of sync with her work. She learned that she has to be extremely careful to whom she exposes her new paintings, that they be people in tune with her sensibility. I have had the same experience with both a painting teacher and a composer with whom I was collaborating on an opera, when both had a very different agenda from my own sensibility and vision.

Then, there is artists' involvement in their own art work in developing an artistic self. Rotenberg (1988) and Hagman (2000) draw upon the formulations of Suzanne Langer (1957) that art is the language most expressive of human experience, and is an objectification of various aspects of the self, of the artist's inner life. They and Milner (1957, 1987) see artists as experiencing their visual artwork as alive and active, and as having transformational influences on the self to the extent that inner puzzles and mental ambiguities are worked out through this externalization. Hagman emphasizes the artist's creative process in which internal and externalized aspects of self-experience enter into a dialectical relationship that transforms both the artwork and the self as the artist strives toward an idealized perfection in the artwork. Milner (1957, 1987) also deals with the artist's interaction with the artwork, viewing it as an idealized, ecstatic product of the imagination, an authentic affective expression, and a creative synthesis between the artist's inner and outer worlds. This does not negate oscillations in the idealization and disillusionment with a given work of art.

There is a further aspect of the artistic self that needs to be considered, Winnicott's notion that the creative artist transcends the depressive phase as the artist has little guilt or concern for others, as well as a great capacity to be in solitude (1958, p. 26). I see Winnicott's ideas as reflecting the observation that when artists are involved in their artwork, they are so deeply absorbed that they do not emotionally relate to others except for those they may be collaborating with. In this sense, artists can be ruthless in their devotion to their work. But they are not ruthless in their relationships. All of the highly recognized career artists in the previous chapter have deep feelings of concern and guilt, of ruth, in their love relationships and friendships – except when it comes to being involved in their art.

There is still another important facet to the artistic self, a cross-cultural one. As Erikson (1950, 1968) and Rank (1932) have noted, the basic psychology of Western man, and in recent decades of women too, is the self-creation of one's identity. This is rooted in various aspects of the culture of individualism in modern Western culture, not the least of which is the enormous autonomy accorded to or thrust upon the individual. This contrasts, for instance, with the essential psychology of traditional Indian culture, which orients persons toward attaining finer inner qualities through following the social etiquette and contextual morality (*dharma*) in complex hierarchical relationships, and ultimately realizing their spiritual self. For the Western artist, as Rank (1932), Menaker (1982), and Brenman-Gibson (1981), an Eriksonian, have delineated, the artist struggles with similar identity issues as others in the society but emerges with a new resolution. From a Rankian perspective, the artist suffers guilt from this increased individuation but assuages it through giving a new aesthetic message to society. In Indian culture, by contrast, the traditional artist affirms the basic values of the society (similar to traditional Japanese and Chinese artists), while the more modern artist serves as an integrating bridge between traditional and Westernizing/modernizing values. Thus, the artistic self of the Western artist is strongly influenced by an individualized self rooted in the culture of individualism.

The artistic self may well be analogized to the spiritual self, which until recent years was seen by Freudian psychoanalysts either as regression to the early infant–mother relationship or as some kind of psychopathology.[7] As the field moved from the reductionistic perspectives of applied psychoanalysis to a new paradigm where psychoanalysts are involved in spiritual disciplines such as meditation, spiritual experiences have been recognized as valid in and of themselves (Coltart, 1992, 1996; Cooper, 1998, 1999; Eigen, 1996; Roland, 1988, 1996, 1999; Rubin, 1996). In one form or another, the spiritual self similar to the artistic self may be inherently present in human beings but only realized by a very few. In both, very particular kinds of transformational objects and selfobjects are needed for this dimension of the self to be actualized. And in both the artist and the mystic, there can also be psychopathology present that interacts with the artistic self and spiritual self in complex ways (see previous chapter and Roland, 1999, respectively).

INHIBITIONS IN THE ARTISTIC SELF

Two-thirds of my patients are either professional career artists or ones who are or have been seriously involved with one or another of the arts. In the previous chapter, I discussed four career artists whose psychological problems involved their artistic career rather than their creative work. This contrasts to other of my patients who strongly aspire to a career in the arts, or who have shown considerable artistic talent, but have a deeply inhibited artistic self.

Philip came to me in his early fifties struggling with being on dialysis for over twenty years. Before then, he was an aspiring television director and writer, who had to abandon his career because of his disability. He mainly did editing work to make an income, supplemented by money his wife made as a professional musician. He very much wanted to get back to his television script writing but couldn't.

Philip had grown up in New England, the oldest son of parents who were of the Haitian aristocracy, but who had fled Haiti because of the political repression. His father was a well-respected science professor at a good college. Philip's identity was one of being white – he was light skinned – of belonging to the intellectual elite, but others usually related to him as being black. As an adolescent, he was expelled from an elite boarding school for a relatively mild prank. He always felt it was because he was seen as black and was therefore discriminated against.

At one point in the therapy, he wondered why his kidneys had failed. I raised the question as to what he felt they couldn't expel or get rid of. Spontaneously he said it was his blackness. He always experienced himself as being white but wanted to get rid of any black blood so he wouldn't be seen as black. Overnight, Philip began to turn out television dramatic scripts and short stories, some of which got aired. By coming to terms with this disavowed aspect of his identity, his artistic self became much freer.

Two other men, Chris and Robert, have also struggled with actualizing their artistic selves. In both cases, each had a mother who was singularly unresponsive and unattuned. They feel that no one would ever listen to anything they would ever write or perform. Small steps in resolving this old object relationship have enabled each to become more involved in his artistic work.

One woman, Christine, a highly successful corporate executive, showed considerable talent as a musician during her childhood and adolescence. She has perfect pitch. However, her father so denigrated her having an artistic career that she turned to a business career, of which he fully approved. However, fantasies have arisen during therapy of buying an expensive violin and playing it at home, which she intends to implement.

THE ARTISTIC PROCESS IN THE THEATER

Most psychoanalysts have focused on artistic creativity primarily in the visual arts and in writing. I would now like to turn to a performing art, the theater, to talk about the artistic process in rehearsals for a play. I shall turn to the perceptive work of both Stephen Aaron (1986), formerly an experienced director with highly creative actors and an acting teacher at the Juilliard Drama Department, who became a psychoanalytically oriented psychologist, and Eric Nuetzel (1995, 1999a, 1999b, 2000), a psychoanalyst who has acted and directed.

Both Aaron and Nuetzel delve into the artistic process and the creative work of actors and directors as they take place during rehearsals, leading up to and including opening night. Both emphasize the imaginative work of actors in developing their characters, as they draw upon various aspects of themselves both conscious and unconscious, and emotional memories. In the process there is an oscillation between the externals of the character's behavior and the inside of the character's personality, which actors must personalize in an authentic way.

While Aaron focuses on the internal work of the actors and their relationship to the director, Nuetzel delineates an unconscious artistic enactment process during rehearsals. As the actors gradually inhabit the play's text, the play's text and characters inhabit them, and they unconsciously enact the characters with each other and with the director in emotional backstage relationships. While this may become problematic at times, it enables actors to become more in touch with emotions that help them deepen the characterization, and which they then incorporate into their acting. Nuetzel also delineates problematic resistances that arise when the actor has an unconscious identification with some troubling aspect of the character. This interferes with the development of the character, but, if resolved, it can deepen the identification with the character.

Aaron cites the major role of the director in the Western theater over the last hundred plus years with the advent of psychological playwrights such as Strindberg, Ibsen, and Pirandello. He describes how the director sets the structure of rehearsals: in the initial phase to play and explore the characters, their motives, and their interactions; in the middle phase for the play to take over; and in the final phase for run-throughs and technical rehearsals, with directors distancing themselves from the actors.

While Nuetzel talks about transferential enactments between actors and the director, Aaron approaches these relationships from an ego psychological understanding. He sees the director taking over ego functions of the actors in terms of memory, attention, reality-testing, self-criticism and self-appraisal, and control of their tension. Descriptively, however, Aaron notes that a director must be empathically in tune with where the actor is at in getting into a role, be careful in his timing to get an actor further into the character, and perform a mirroring function to affirm what the actor has done that is worthwhile particularly in the first phase of rehearsals. The director thus performs as a transformational object to the actor's artistic self as the latter develops the character. Actors have no one but the director to confirm their development of their characters into a performing, artistic self.

As Nuetzel, influenced by self psychology as well as traditional psychoanalysis, notes, the director is both an idealized figure to the actor as well as a crucial mirroring one to the actor's developing, performing self. Nuetzel further adds the director's alter-ego relationship with the actor, as the former identifies with each of the characters of the play. One can add that actors also have alter-ego relationships with each other.

Stage fright, the centerpiece of Aaron's work, is seen as primarily the actor's separation anxiety from the director in facing the audience with a character that draws upon various facets of one's own self for authenticity but which is also different from oneself. Highly talented actors often have enormous stage fright, and it is usually only the actor with a modicum of talent that is free from it. Aaron sees stage fright as significantly greater than the anxiety of other performing artists – musicians, dancers, and such – because of the actor presenting a character that is paradoxically both different from and similar to oneself. Besides separation anxiety from the director, Aaron analyzes other components of stage fright as deriving from guilt over sexuality, aggression, exhibitionism, anal-sadistic and oral-feeding fantasies, and phallic-Oedipal ones. Stage fright disappears upon the actor's contact with the audience, even a disapproving one.

Stage fright may also be seen from other perspectives than the generalized separation anxiety due to the loss of the director. More specifically, it is losing the director as a transformational object, as well as a mirroring figure attuned to and affirming the artistic self of the actor as a particular character. The anxiety is one of self-fragmentation, more specifically, the fragmentation of the artistic self. But it goes beyond this. Toward the end of rehearsals when directors distance themselves, actors have created their characters as a unique expression of their artistic self. As Aaron notes, the character is now their own. There can be enormous anxiety until a new responsive object appears, the audience. As the audience responds to the play and its characters, the actor's artistic self becomes affirmed and the anxiety of its self-fragmentation disappears ... only to reoccur the following evening when there is a new audience.

As a footnote to the artistic process in the theater, one should add the playwright and the text as important idealized figures. (Personal communication from Frederick Feirstein, a playwright, poet, and psychoanalyst.) They serve an important function to the artistic self of both the actor and director to do the play well. If the text is misinterpreted by a given director, as occasionally happens, it affects the artistic self of the actors.

DEVELOPMENT OF AN ARTISTIC SELF

My interest in this topic was stimulated from working with patients such as Marjorie and Angela as well as Hal and John, from personal experiences in the arts, and from observations over the years of my son, Ari, a professional jazz musician in the bebop tradition. In fact, my initial ideas on this subject came from working with Marjorie in psychoanalytic therapy. It was striking to me as she described her work with a well-known choreographer who created his best work with Marjorie as his director. It became evident that Marjorie was in tune with this person's artistic self in a way no other director has been before or since. Marjorie was a crucial mirroring figure with him as she has been with other artists as well. While this was in dance, it is obviously related to work in the theater where some directors can bring out actors more than others.

I would like to turn to long-term observations of my son, Ari, to describe how artists' transformational objects and selfobjects played out for him in his eventually becoming a well-regarded, full-time, professional jazz musician. From the age of 9 until his early twenties, he had an extraordinarily close alter-ego relationship with a friend, another talented musician. Within a couple of years they went from playing rock music to fusion to the jazz bebop tradition. They spent all of their spare time for years playing together, listening to jazz bebop tapes, or talking passionately about jazz and various bebop musicians. I shall never forget one summer when at age 14 they helped me remove the debris from a fallen shed. Not for five minutes during the six hours we worked together did they stop talking about jazz! It was clear to me that this alter-ego friendship was crucial for both of them in their development of an artistic self as jazz musicians.

Ari and his friend have had a number of deceased jazz musicians as idealized selfobjects, most of them within the bebop tradition. Foremost by far for both is Charlie Parker although neither Ari nor his friend plays the saxophone. For Ari, who plays the double bass, it has been Israel Crosby, a renowned bass player, together with two or three others. He has listened over and over again to everything Parker and Crosby have recorded, and they still serve as inspiration. However, it is also important to note that there are other major jazz musicians, living and dead, who serve as markers to be avoided, and who also help define his artistic self. They do not accord well with his musical sensibility or the bebop tradition to which he adheres.

There were also living idealized musicians within the bebop tradition, some of them teachers, who also served as mirroring selfobjects. One in particular was a renowned bebop pianist-teacher. Others for Ari were a group of outstanding, underground bebop jazz musicians with whom he started playing at age 14. Some of them were apparently great musicians who never made it commercially because of drug and/or alcohol addiction, or simply refusing to go on tour, sometimes turning down lucrative contracts. A few of them served as important mentors to his developing artistic self as a jazz musician. They were never easy on him, at times being downright critical, but that is also part of the tradition.

He then had a classical bass teacher from the Juilliard Pre-College Program and the Juilliard School, to whom he was referred by one of his jazz mentors for training in classical bowing technique, something at which few jazz bassists are adept. I noticed that there was a reciprocal selfobject relationship going on that probably is present in all artistic mentoring. On the one hand, Ari clearly idealized his teacher and tried to live up to his expectations, thus enhancing his own artistic self; on the other hand, it became clear that his teacher's self-esteem was profoundly tied up with how well his pupils were performing. Thus, each was a selfobject for the other but in a different way.

Eventually, there were other important factors that led to a further development of his artistic self. He had played in clubs with his friend for years, who has also become a well-regarded, full-time professional jazz musician. Then one day, an old-time drummer, whom Ari greatly respected, invited him to play with his group but not his friend. This was a very important affirmation that Ari could be artistically recognized as independent of his friend. Equally important, after years of mentoring, he began developing his own musical ideas and style of playing, departing from those of his teachers. To get to another artistic level, he felt he had to forego some of the important ways of his previous mentors who had been absolutely crucial to the development of his artistic self. A further step in consolidating his artistic self has been to play professionally only in the bebop tradition, and only with musicians who have attained a high level of musicianship within this tradition.

CONCLUSIONS

Self psychology and object relations theory afford other perspectives on the psychology of the artist. I have formulated an artistic self with its own sensibilities, resonances, history, organization, and particular needs for transformational objects and selfobjects. The artistic tradition(s) in a given art field to which an artist is drawn by sensibility and talent, and within which one works, encompasses the more usual kinds of transformational and selfobject relationships – mentoring, mirroring, idealizing, and alter-ego ones. This would also be true of the artwork, itself. All of these relationships are crucial to the development, functioning, and maintenance of the artistic self. A cross-cultural perspective adds another dimension to understanding the artistic self.

NOTES

1.   There is an appreciable difference between self psychology and object relations theory on the nature of idealizing relationships. The former sees the need for idealized figures as central to the development, enhancement, and maintenance of self-esteem and self-cohesiveness. Whereas the latter views idealizing relationships as always involving a defense against underlying ambivalence and anger, as well as a need to preserve the object. Clinically, with a multi-model orientation, one often sees both kinds of idealization to be simultaneously present, one kind more in

focus than the other at any given phase in the therapy. Therapeutic interventions then depend on making this kind of assessment.

2. The art historian, Rose Washton Long (2001), cites the German artists, Lucia Moholy and Laszio Mohly-Nagy, who were each more creative in their photography while married than either was before their marriage or after their divorce.
3. Relational psychoanalysis has both a general and a specific meaning. It broadly refers to various schools of psychoanalysis that are oriented toward a two-person psychology, taking into account the subjectivity of the analyst as well as the patient, in contrast to the traditional Freudian orientation to a one-person psychology, the patient. More specifically, relational psychoanalysis initially developed at the Relational Track of the New York University Postdoctoral Program in Psychoanalysis and Psychotherapy. It was originally a synthesis of Sullivanian interpersonal psychoanalysis from the William Alanson White Institute and British object relations theory.
4. This is even more striking because American women are seen as having a self that is significantly more relational than American men (Gilligan, 1980).
5. I am indebted to Frederick Feirstein for emphasizing the importance of traditions for the artist in their art field.
6. Asian metonymic thinking, in contrast to Western symbolic thinking, can be illustrated by statues or icons of gods or holy figures. In symbolic thinking, a statue of an Indian goddess would be seen as a symbolic representation of that goddess. But in metonymic thinking, the statue is considered an actual partial manifestation of the goddess.
7. Bollas's (1987) notion of aesthetic experience as an existential recollection of the infant–mother relationship has much in common with the reductionism that has characterized the psychoanalytic view of the spiritual self. Both rest on the faulty assumption that an egoless experience without thoughts must invariably be a recollection of the pre-verbal infant–mother relationship rather than an adult existential state of being. Certain nonverbal and non-thought adult experiences are not necessarily a regression to the pre-verbal.

PART II

Dreams, Imagery, and Creativity

3

The Context and Unique Function of Dreams in Psychoanalytic Therapy

INTRODUCTION

From close scrutiny of the dream literature and working with dreams in psychoanalytic therapy, the problem of the context in which dreams are reported in psychoanalysis and the function they serve in the ongoing therapy need important amplification. While the clinical approach to dreams expressed in this chapter is obviously practiced by some analysts, it has not to my knowledge been given a sound enough theoretical basis or been described sufficiently in the dream literature. By clarification and elaboration of the context and the bases for the unique function of dreams, I hope to contribute towards a better conceptualized approach in working with dreams in psychoanalytic therapy.

Such an approach has added relevance because of an increasing controversy over the place of the dream in psychoanalysis. One school of thought (Arlow and Brenner, 1964; Waldhorn, 1967) diminishes the importance of dreams, designating them on the same order of psychic value as the various other means of communication in psychoanalysis, such as free associations, fantasy, transference phenomena, and so forth. As reported by Altman (1969), this downgrading of the dream seems to have gained a widespread hearing in many American psychoanalytic training institutes. Another school of thought (Kanzer, 1955; Bergmann, 1966; Klauber, 1967) opts for the uniqueness of the dream, not so much because of its being the royal road to the unconscious, but rather because of its communicative function in the ongoing therapy. Altman (1969), as a dissenting member of the Kris Study Group (Waldhorn, 1967), joined this other group in stressing the importance of the dream for psychoanalysis. Greenson (1970) has stressed the exceptional place of the dream because it reveals with unusual clarity various aspects of psychic structure and functions, dynamics, genetic material, and economic considerations.

RELEVANT CONTEXT

The first concept that needs better conceptualization for dream interpretation is that of the 'context.' Freud (1900) early recognized the need to know a great deal about the dreamer's life situation in order to interpret a dream; in other words, any interpretation of a dream must take place in the context of the dreamer's ongoing life situation and/or therapy. His conceptualization of context was mainly in terms of instigators of a dream, i.e. significant events or thoughts that seemed to cause a particular dream. This he differentiated from the day residue, where innocuous events of the previous day or two are often incorporated into a dream. Altman (1969) uses the concept 'context' in various places in his book, stressing how context affects interpretation. Throughout much, but not all, of the dream literature, the general importance of context for interpretation is noted, but in none of the literature is context ever dealt with or conceptualized in any systematic manner. As a result, I have found in talking with a number of analysts and looking carefully through the literature that there is great variation in the extent to which an analyst takes into account the context in interpreting a dream, and still further variation in terms of how the context is used.

What I would like to stress first is the need for the relevant context, and its crucial importance in dream interpretation. A simple example will illustrate this, the Irma dream of Freud. In *The Interpretation of Dreams* (1900) Freud cites the instigator or context of the dream as Otto's possible criticism of Freud's treatment of Irma. But in a later reworking of the Irma dream by Erikson (1954), the relevant context is seen much more basically as Freud's coming to the monumental discovery of the very meaning of the dream itself. It becomes readily apparent from a close reading of the two accounts how great a difference the noting of the relevant context alone makes in the interpretive approach to the Irma dream, notwithstanding the other differences in the two interpretive orientations. However, this example also indicates that there may be related subsidiary contexts to the relevant one.

In my experience, the search for the relevant context is often a rather difficult task. As much energetic thought is necessary in trying to judge the psychical problem currently in focus to which the dream is addressing itself as in deciphering the dream itself. While the relevant context is often enough in the foreground of the transference situation or important life events of the patient, at other times it is some seemingly peripheral matter, or may be a developing transference that does not become evident until days or weeks after the dream. Some analysts contend that once the transference neurosis is established, the relevant context is always related to the transference neurosis. My experience indicates that this is very often, but definitely not always, the case. Further, that even when the relevant context is related to the transference neurosis, it still may be rather difficult to ascertain.

Because of the importance of finding the relevant context, I would stress the necessity for the analyst to search for it at the same time that he and the patient may be delving into the associations and meanings of the dream. For once the relevant context is established, the dream becomes very much easier to work with. From careful observation of every patient's dream and the context in which it arose over a year's time (1967–68), and from supervising other therapists, it is my distinct impression that the inaccessibility of many dreams is due far less to the patient's resistance than to the therapist not noting the relevant context. At times, it has even been helpful in asking patients what they think the dream is relevant to, in order to arrive at the context.

With regard to the psychology of the context, I hypothesize that it is more closely related to the psychology of remembering and reporting dreams in analysis than to the instigator of the dream, although context and instigator may often coincide. This conceptualization is borne out by the phenomena that dreams from days or even weeks previously are not infrequently reported after a therapist gives an interpretation or poses a question. Here the relevant context for interpretation is not the dream instigator, or other events around the time of the dream, but rather the very interpretation or question that the analyst raised. My hypothesis is thus in accord with Klauber's (1967) important work emphasizing the metapsychological processes in the reporting of dreams. It also recognizes the research findings in rapid-eye-movement sleep, from which it became apparent that the number of dreams reported in analysis are but a small fraction of those dreamt each night. Thus for dream interpretation we must constantly question why a dream has been reported at this or that particular time during the analysis. In this respect our focus shifts from what gave rise to a dream (the dream instigator) to considering what a dream is addressing itself or is relevant to (the communicative dimension).

DREAM AS UNIQUE COMMUNICATION

The second point that needs important amplification and better conceptualization concerns the uniqueness of the dream for psycho-analytic therapy. From my own study of dream material in psycho-analytic therapy, it became apparent that, if finding the relevant context is crucial for the interpretation of the dream, then the dream itself has a unique contribution to make towards the understanding of the particular relevant context or emotional problem to which the dream is related. In emphasizing the dream as communication, as has Klauber, Bergmann, and Kanzer, I see the dream as able to shed more light on a given context or psychical problem than other communications in psychoanalysis because of one major factor and two interrelated subsidiary ones.

My observations indicate that the dream is the only communication in psychoanalytic therapy with the incipient makings of a paradox,[1] which can then be realized through creative interpretive work to illuminate more effectively than other communications the psychical problem (relevant context) in focus. By this I mean that after we are successfully able to analyze a dream in relation to its relevant context, i.e. upon closer scrutiny of the total dream in its multifaceted symbolic expression, the latent content falls into two basic structural elements (in terms of structural linguistics) of seeming opposites or contradictions. In other words, after the associations are obtained, and after our knowledge of primary-process mechanisms is utilized, our interpreta-tions always seem to integrate opposites into statements effectively explaining the relevant context. Thus dreams have the makings of effective paradoxes, where contradictory lines of thought are synthe-sized into a fuller truth related to the relevant context.

Here it is important to differentiate my concept of structural opposites existing in the latent content only, from the more well-known observations of opposites or contradictions as coexisting in the manifest content; or of certain aspects of the latent content being the opposite of part of the manifest content through the primary-process mechanism of displacement. I must further differentiate and relate my observation of structural opposites in the latent content from the obvious presence and depiction of conflict and ambivalence in dreams. My observations indicate (which I shall illustrate below) that structural opposites in the latent content often, but by no means always, coincide with conflict and only sometimes coincide with ambivalence

Two interrelated factors contribute crucially to the manifestation of structural opposites in the latent content, and thus to the uniqueness of the dream. The first is the ability of the ego[2] to give symbolic expression[3] to the various structures, functions, dynamics, ego and self states, memories, internalizations, and early object relations of the psyche. This is done through the primary-process mechanisms of displacement, condensation, symbolization (in the classical usage), and means of representation. From my observations, and in accordance with Deri's (1984) important work on symbolization, I find primary-process mechanisms in the dream serve a dual function. To the extent that the various mechanisms of the primary process are related to wish-fulfillment, they serve the purpose as stated in the classical psycho-analytic literature of enabling the unconscious wish to evade the superego for expression. Here the primary process is in the service of disguised expression because of the superego, anxiety, and defensive operations. However, when these mechanisms are related to the various psychic structures, to the internalizations of the ego and self and superego, to internal object relations and self states, and to the processes and functions of the ego, they serve to give them a rich symbolic expression, depicting just where the psyche is at with regard to various conflicts. Thus the primary process here is in the service of symbolic expression and good symbolic fit, rather than disguise and distortion. This emphasis on symbolic expression rather than disguise is in accord with the development of psychoanalytic theory from an id psychology, with its correlated emphasis on wish-fulfillment in dreams, to the later structural hypothesis and ego psychology as well as object relations theory, self psychology, and intersubjectivity, where interest centers on the various structures and ego processes, and on internal objects and aspects of the self in dreams, as well as on wish-fulfillment. My observations on the primary process in dreams are closely in accord with Noy's (1969) important paper that primary process is best defined by its function, which is both the integration of new experiences into the self and the ability to give expression to the various aspects of the self, rather than dealing with outer reality which is the function of the secondary process, and to Deri's (1984) seminal book on the rich symbolization of the primary process to give expression to various aspects of the psyche.

The second factor follows closely from the first. The dream through its superior symbolic expression, more than any other expression of psychical life (with the possible exception of art), is able to give simultaneous expression to totally different, often conflicting structures, drives, affects, and layers of personality, including various internalizations or aspects of self, all from different stages of development which can usually gain only a one-sided hearing in other communications; or which may be synthesized beyond recognition in symptoms or character traits. This second factor is then a more explicit elaboration of some of Freud's thoughts on ego fragmentation in dreams (1923a), and particularly of Federn's (1952) positing the simultaneous expression of different ego states in a single dream, which is usually not possible in other expressions of the psyche. This multifaceted expression in dreams is also in keeping with Greenson's paper (1970), which pointed out the many-sided aspects of the psyche a single dream can express, and with Bollas's (1987) emphasis on both the thematic and aesthetic style in dreams.

In summary, the dream as communication may be viewed as a multifaceted symbolic expression,[4] which is composed in the latent content of structural opposites. When these opposites are integrated through creative interpretive work in relation to the relevant context, a much fuller understanding of the psychical problem in focus becomes possible than through other communications.

EXAMPLE OF A DREAM

At this point an example of a dream is in order to illustrate my overall interpretive approach interrelating relevant context with the dream as a multifaceted symbolic expression with structural opposites in the latent content. The dream is that of a 21-year-old girl, Jane, who had come from Boston to New York City for college, and who had been in psychoanalytic therapy just less than a year at the time of the dream. In this particular example, the relevant context was quite easy to arrive at in contrast to other dreams that could be cited. The relevant context was her bringing her boyfriend, Charles, home to her parents and brother for the first time, with a considerable reaction of little understood anxiety that the visit home would somehow completely sabotage her current good relationship with Charles. The dream was reported after a stage in therapy of working on her pervasive reaction of apathy when visiting home. It had become apparent and was interpreted to her that she was caught in a conflict where strong dependency needs on her parents prevented her from striving towards autonomy and individualization due to the parents' striking inability to allow any self-assertion without cutting off their relationship with her. These interpretations enabled her to become somewhat more self-assertive in striving towards her own identity.

Jane's dream

I am driving in a section of North Boston. It's full of violence and I'm afraid. I'm following my brother in his car [a sports car], but not too closely. I don't want him to know I'm following him. [On later inquiry, she associated that she was afraid to follow him too closely in childhood, as he didn't want her tagging after him.] I'm hoping he'll lead the way out. Then, I remember I'm to meet Charles at the train station and I'm afraid I'll be late and miss the train and him.

Upon further questioning her for description of the dream scene, she recognized that the surroundings were very similar to the neighborhood she grew up in as a young child, another section of Boston. She then spontaneously associated that North Boston is in reality an African-American neighborhood in contrast to the area she had lived in. She further described the people on the streets as being silently and sullenly violent, with much pent-up rage.

My interpretive approach to the dream tried to relate the relevant context (her intense anxiety over the effect of the visit home on the relationship with Charles) to the dream, and to use the dream as a multifaceted expression of opposites to clarify the anxiety, or the relevant context.[5] Before describing the interpretive work, it is first necessary to delineate the dream as a multifaceted symbolic expression, with its structural opposites in the latent content. In doing this, we will also allude to the dual use of the primary process as giving both disguised and rich symbolic expression of the psyche.

In the first part of the dream, to summarize, great anxiety was depicted over intense feelings of repressed rage (the silent and sullenly violent blacks with pent-up rage) from childhood (the old neighborhood). Also depicted through the blacks is a passive, subservient childhood adaptation with a self-image of the victim. From the standpoint of the primary process, it is apparent that through the mechanism of displacement disguised expression and fulfillment is given to Jane's feelings of rage. However, in terms of the symbolic expression of the primary process, this displacement also represents accurately through ego-distancing (discussed below) the defensive and repressive operations of the ego. Moreover, the fact that her rage is represented by many others rather than by one indicates its intensity; and her reaction of fear to the blacks also shows anxiety over the repressed rage becoming expressed. Through condensation, the image of the silently and sullenly violent blacks with much pent-up rage not only aids in the disguised expression of the rage, but also gives excellent symbolic expression of the nature of her reaction to rigidly enforced compliance by her parents, of her masochistic self-image with being the subservient underdog at home, and of her repressed rage threatening current good relationships.

In the next part of the dream, there is a fearful wish of following the brother's example at home of open rebellion (as much as she was compelled to be subservient, he was subtly encouraged to be rebellious) as a way out of her subservience and repressed rage. On a psychosexual level the wish to express the phallic urges (following his car) and penis envy of the brother are also present. The dual use of the primary process can again be seen through the image of her following the brother's car, who is leading the way out. Here, through the symbol of the car (in the classic psychoanalytic sense), there is disguised expression of phallic strivings and penis envy. But also given symbolic expression is the brother as ego ideal, an ideal of actual rebellion in the family that might represent a way out from enforced compliance with its resultant destructive rage. Further represented through her associations is her fear of following too closely in his footsteps, i.e. the fear of being the rebellious girl giving expression to her phallic urges. Finally, in the third part of the dream there is the fear of missed communication and a breakup of the relationship with Charles (missing Charles's train – Kanzer, 1955).

Having summarized the multifaceted symbolic expression of this dream, I will now differentiate the structural opposites in the latent content from the conflicts depicted. Conflict in the dream revolves around a masochistic (Menaker, 1953) passive-subservient adaptation from childhood with repressed rage, as against more open self-assertion and rebellion. This conflict has been dynamically maintained because of internalized images of the parents as cutting off their love relationship with her if there was any self-assertion on her part. The conflict further manifests in the area of sexual identity, where penis envy and anxiety over phallic strivings are present. Still another conflict in the dream concerns the possible breaking through of the rage to actual manifestation. However, the structural opposites that must be integrated for interpretive work are the anxiety over the repressed rage on one hand, and the fear of the breakup of her love relationship with Charles on the other. Putting it in a more literary mode of expression, rage and love are juxtaposed, and form the elements of a possible paradox that must clarify the intense anxiety over the effects of visiting home expressed in the relevant context.

The interpretive work pointed out to Jane that she was afraid that her visit home with Charles would reestablish the old forms of masochistic relationship with her parents in the context of some newly won self-assertion. This in turn would reevoke intense reactions of rage from childhood, with considerable anxiety that the rage might spill over into her relationship with Charles, the only good one she had, thus wrecking it. Further, that the one way out she could now visualize in the dream was to follow in her brother's footsteps by being more rebellious at home. Here it should be mentioned that while the immediate interpretive work tried to interrelate dream and relevant context, the dream could be and was used for further later investigative and interpretive work on such issues as the specific nature of the masochistic relationship with each parent, the dual roles of the two children at home, and the envy of the brother. It is interesting to note that two years after the dream, the intense rage depicted in the dream began to manifest in the transference neurosis, with far more self-assertive behavior in her relationships with others.

SYMBOLIC EXPRESSION IN DREAMS

In the preceding section I have attempted to describe my approach in interrelating the relevant context with the dream as a multifaceted symbolic expression of opposites. At this point, I would like to amplify briefly two contributions importantly related to symbolic expression in dreams, which I believe have not received significant emphasis in the dream literature. The first is the concept of ego-distancing, which originated with Tomkins (1947) in his work on the Thematic Apperception Test, and was further developed by Sheppard and Saul (1958) differentiating dreams of psychotics from those of neurotics and normals. Ego-distancing relates to the degree to which the dreamer portrays his impulses as not being a part of himself in the dream because of anxiety and defensive operations. It also relates to the degree to which the ego is impaired in its various functions. As illustrated in Jane's dream (the blacks with pent-up rage), the primary-process mechanism of displacement integrated with the concept of ego-distancing gives a fuller description of the defensive operations of the ego.

Taking into account ego-distancing, the full use of the human, animal, and inanimate environment in their interaction in dreams becomes invaluable for interpretation. Thus, to arrive at the fact that another person or animal or object or movements in a dream represent specific aspects of the dreamer's psyche through displacement is only of limited importance for interpretation. It must be further ascertained to what extent these symbolic expressions are motivated defensively or not through ego-distancing. Thus in Jane's dream the rage-filled blacks was a displacement defensively motivated, while the section of North Boston was mainly a displacement symbolically expressive of a childhood ego state.

An important qualification must be added about the relationship of ego-distancing to the mechanisms of defense. It appears too simple a process to state that because another person or animal or object in a dream embodies important aspects of the dreamer's psyche that this is primarily due to the specific defenses of projection or displacement, as one sometimes sees in the literature. Since all aspects of the dream are expressions in one way or another of the psyche of the dreamer, these displacements (primary process) appear to be due to the symbolization process. Thus close scrutiny of the dream and a good knowledge of the dreamer is required to identify accurately the actual mechanisms of defense operating. In Jane's dream, at that period of the analysis, the reaction of rage to the parents was largely repressed, and did come out occasionally in displaced (defense) reactions to her boyfriend. With other patients, I have noted displacements (primary process) in dreams that were defensively motivated as being related to the ego defenses of projection and ego-splitting.

The second contribution related to symbolic expression in dreams is the need for greater attention to be paid to the manifest content in psychoanalytic therapy, a point of view first promulgated by Erikson (1954) and elaborated upon by Deri (1984) and Bollas (1987). As Erikson, Deri, and Bollas indicated, this is not at variance with Freud's work in arriving at the latent dream thoughts, but rather complements it, and even furthers it, as I shall indicate. An important approach towards the fullest use of the manifest content is by getting the patient to cathect the boundaries of the total dream more fully by encouraging him to pay more serious attention to the dream image. This can be accomplished by having him give a much fuller description of the dream than is ordinarily given in session (Deri, 1984). A therapist can simply ask a patient to describe the dream image in as much detail as possible, even after the dream has been reported.

Not only does this usually bring to light many other facets of the dream than were initially reported, but time and again the very reporting of the image in detail leads to important, relevant associations and memories that point the way to the latent dream thoughts. This approach is often far more effective in getting relevant associations than the classical method of asking the patient to associate to different parts of the dream, though both methods can obviously be used to supplement each other.[6] Paradoxically, by paying more careful attention to the "surface" of the dream, one can reach the depth meanings, or latent content, more easily. This can be seen in Jane's dream where inquiring for a fuller description of the dream scene not only led to its association to a childhood ego state (a neighborhood she grew up in before the age of 9), but to a much richer description of her self (the underdog African-American, silently and sullenly violent, with pent-up rage). It should also be noted that the nonhuman environment in its specific aspects in a dream (e.g. the neighborhood with its particular streets and houses as representing a childhood ego state) often lends itself to important symbolic expression, and often needs a fuller elaboration than is usually initially given.

THEORETICAL DISCUSSION: REVIEW OF THE RELEVANT DREAM LITERATURE

A review of some of the literature on dreams seems in order to show points of contact, with similarities and differences in approach between this book and others. Freud's (1900) views on context and those elaborated here have already been discussed (above). With regard to dream imagery, Freud (1900) may be said to have formulated two theories of why the manifest content is different from the latent dream thoughts. The one on which he laid the most emphasis was the necessity of disguised expression through the primary-process mechanisms of displacement, condensation, and symbolization for the infantile, unconscious wish to evade the dream censor (in later formulations, the superego). The second theory, upon which much less emphasis was placed, was the means of representation, i.e. that the manifest content had to represent underlying thoughts and meanings in a basically pictorial manner, which was far more metaphorical and symbolically expressive in nature than more rational, scientific, secondary-process thinking. This latter theory of the manifest content was further elaborated by Sharpe (1937), who took great pains to show that the means of representation include various aspects of poetic diction in visual form, including the dramatization of different aspects of the psyche. Bollas (1987) further elaborated the ego's aesthetic style in the manifest content as expressing the early mother–child relationship, while Ornstein (1987) described self-state dreams. It is basically towards Freud's second theory of the manifest content that this present discussion is oriented, recognizing with Sharpe that the symbolical expressiveness of the pictorial manifest content is eminently suited to give representation to very different aspects of the psyche. We may now add that these different aspects fall into structural opposites in the latent content and can be interpretively integrated relating to the relevant context.

There are two important issues connected with the above that must be discussed. One is Freud's seeming ambivalence, or perhaps lack of conceptual clarity, with regard to dreams being a multifaceted expression of the psyche. In 1900 he talks of the composite nature[7] of dreams. However, in 1923a, while recognizing ego fragmentation in dreams, particularly in connection with different persons in a dream often representing different aspects of the dreamer's psyche, he then minimizes it.[8] Here we must respectfully disagree with Freud's apparently minimizing ego fragmentation in dreams by his putting it on an equal basis with ego fragmentation in daily life. In my observations, it is just because ego fragmentation in dreams is of such a different order than in conscious, daily life, through representation of highly varied and often conflicting aspects of the psyche, that the dream is of such enormous value.

The second issue is that of Freud's description of the pictorial qualities of the manifest content as stemming from more regressive, primary-process visual thinking of childhood. From this point of view, an orientation has arisen that pervades the dream literature that pictorial thinking and the primary process is more regressive, archaic, primitive, infantile, and inferior to more adult, rational, conceptual, verbal, and scientific secondary-process thinking. The assumptions that underlie such a characterization are now open to serious question, and are discussed in detail in the next chapter. Moreover, a well-conceptualized, alternative approach in defining the primary process by its function as relating to the integration and expression of the self has been presented by Noy (1969) and elaborated upon by Deri (1984). It is important to recognize that pictorial representation in dreams is not simply visual in nature but, as Freud first recognized and Sharpe emphasized, is highly metaphorical and symbolically expressive as well. Similar to Sharpe, Bollas (1987), McDougall (1991), and Milner (1987) see the dream as a creative and dramatic process. This mode of thinking is of course far more literary and artistic in nature, where metaphorical thinking is based on visual imagery, than are the simple, concrete visual images of childhood. *Rather than being inferior to rational, secondary-process thinking, symbolically expressive thinking of a metaphorical nature,*[9] *using primary-process mechanisms, is intrinsically far better suited to represent simultaneously and in depth a far broader spectrum of psychic life than other more rational modes, and becomes the basis for meaningful and valuable paradoxes.* This is one of the basic factors upon which rests the great value of the dream for psychoanalytic therapy. It further supports Freud's great emphasis on the dream as the richest communication about psychic life.

It is because the structural and ego psychological approaches (Arlow and Brenner, 1964; Waldhorn, 1967) minimize so greatly the nature of pictorial metaphorical thinking that they on the one hand so under-estimate the value of the dream for psychoanalytic therapy, and on the other hand do not see its great relevance in terms of their own approach to the structural hypothesis and the principle of multiple functioning. This chapter differs from the aforementioned writers in the observation that the multiple functioning of psychic structures are given far better representation and expression in dreams than in other communications through the ego's multifaceted symbolic expression. My viewpoint is also in accord with their position that dreams must be related to the context of the overall psychoanalytic situation, but the clinical examples of the Kris Study Group (Waldhorn, 1967) did not convey any systematic investigation of relevant contexts.

A whole other approach to dreams, that of their communicative nature, is highly relevant to this chapter's argument and deserves careful comment. This approach started with Ferenczi (1913) and received greater impetus with Kanzer (1955), Bergmann (1966), and Klauber (1967). In this orientation the remembering and telling of a dream is viewed as an urge to communicate to another person. Kanzer indicated that dreams give important evidence of urges to communicate as well as difficulties in communication, particularly as these become manifest in the transference. Bergmann further elaborated on this viewpoint by distinguishing between the intrapsychic nature of a dream (i.e. learning about the dreamer's personality) and the communicative function, noting that in this latter aspect dreams are often hidden communications to the analyst about the transference or psychoanalytic situation, or may even portray a conflict which cannot be expressed in any other way. Klauber delved further into the psychology of reporting dreams in therapy by hypothesizing: (a) that the reported dream is a result of the ego's attempt to communicate to the analyst for assistance its own attitude towards an underlying conflict; (b) that the dream is necessarily related to current reality, the analytic transference, and the future in terms of wish-fulfillment; and (c) that dreams not only defensively cover up, but also are willing to express derivatives for communication.

It is clear that the basic viewpoint of this chapter's argument is in total agreement with the approach that dreams are reported in psychoanalytic therapy as an important urge to communicate for the analyst's assistance, and give important evidence thereto. My orientation, similar to Klauber's, stresses the total dream as communication related to the patient's analysis and/or life situation, with particular stress on the dream's relationship to the relevant context. Thus, we do not make nearly so sharp a distinction as Bergmann does between the intrapsychic and communicative aspects of a dream, rather seeing them as being closely interwoven. On the theoretical basis of why dreams have something special to communicate, Klauber emphasizes the irradiation of hidden areas of the psyche by crude energies displaced towards them, with an attempt of the ego to define an attitude towards the psychic conflicts. I stress the ability of the ego to give symbolic expression to different sides of the psyche in conflict, manifesting in structural opposites related to the relevant context. These two views are not necessarily in conflict, but may be complementary.

In some ways, the most relevant and provocative approach to dreams for this chapter is that of French and Fromm (1964), more recently elaborated upon by Fosshage (1987). Here there is a good example of differing approaches towards use of the relevant context. While they clearly note it, French and Fromm work completely on interpretation of the dream first, and only then use the relevant context or precipitating emotional situation as a means to check their hypotheses about the dream. This is in contrast to the approach here where the search for the relevant context goes on simultaneously with exploration of the dream, and is then used in approaching the dream for interpretation. Probably more crucial than this, French and Fromm see dreams as efforts to solve psychological problems, with the dream work as hierarchical substitutions by analogy or metaphor of one problem for another, motivated by wish-fulfillment and/or defensive avoidance of facing focal conflicts. I agree with their view of the analogous or metaphorical picturing of psychical conflicts in the dream, and their noting that this way of thinking is basically different from verbal thinking with syntactical structure. But I rather see these so-called substitutions not as basically problem-solving or as a defensive avoidance of such, but rather as multifaceted symbolic expressions to communicate the problem to the analyst, expressions that are usually of a contradictory or paradoxical nature. Thus my emphasis is more on symbolic fit and communicative expressiveness rather than on problem-solving or avoidance of the central problem. This dimension is more in line with the communicative function of the dream as discussed above.

NOTES

1. The comparison of dreams and art on paradox and poetic metaphor is discussed in the next chapter.
2. We consider the production of imagery to be a basic ego function through which the various aspects of the psyche are expressed.
3. We define symbolic expression here in terms of the total imagery that gives expression to the multiple aspects and structures of the psyche. Symbolic expression is a broader concept than the classic psychoanalytic definition of symbolism, which is a substitute formation of certain aspects of the id. Symbolic expression as used here encompasses symbolism but is not limited to it.
4. To some extent the synthetic function of the ego in its differentiating aspect is related to multifaceted symbolic expression. However, we view the latter as going well beyond what is expressed by the concept of differentiation.
5. It is important to note that our interpretive approach has been found applicable not only to dreams from our own patients, but to those reported by supervisees and even to those well described in the literature, such as in Greenson's paper (1970). While Greenson obviously did not use our conceptual framework, his actual analytic work fits to a considerable extent within it.
6. It is important to stress that no single method can substitute for the sensitive, cooperative associative work on both patient's and analyst's part that Greenson (1970) so well describes. However, knowledge of different approaches can definitely aid in such work.
7. "Dreams . . . as being of a composite character, as being conglomerates of psychical formations."
8. "In itself this multiplicity [of the ego in dreams] is no more remarkable than the multiple appearance of the ego in a waking thought, especially when the ego divides itself into subject and object, puts one part of itself as an observing and critical agency in contrast to the other, or compares its present nature with its recollected past, which was also ego once . . ."
9. Here we use metaphorical thinking in the more popularized manner of one mode of expression representing another, rather than as poetic metaphor which joins together two different levels of experience, such as concrete and abstract.

4

Imagery and Symbolic Expression in Dreams and Art

CULTURAL ATTITUDES AND SYMBOLIZATION

In any serious discussion of the psychoanalytic theory of imagery and symbolic expression in dreams and art, it is first necessary to point out that the psychoanalytic literature is pervaded by the characterization that metaphorical thinking[1] in particular, and the primary process in general, are more primitive, inferior and regressive as compared with abstract, conceptual secondary-process thinking. This characterization rests in part on the basic assumption that, both historically and individually, the development of language and thinking is from the metaphorical to the conceptual. The psychoanalytic literature, beginning with Freud (1900), then with important contributions by Rank and Sachs (1913), and Jones (1916), on through contemporary psychoanalysis including the English school, is replete with this basic assumption.

Related to the primary process and metaphorical thinking is the important problem of symbol-formation and symbolization. In the early literature, symbol-formation and symbolization (Jones, 1916) was further considered to be inferior due to intellectual or affective inhibition, mainly the latter. Symbolization was conceptualized as part of the primary process, thus being in the service of the pleasure principle, and as developing only to give expression to inhibited feelings or drives that would otherwise have no other means of representation. This viewpoint was then extended to metaphorical thinking in general.

With the development of ego psychology and the adaptive point of view in psychoanalysis, some way was sought to include the obvious positive features of metaphorical thinking and poetic metaphor, such as in art. Writers like Kris (1952) and Milner (1952) still rested on the assumption that metaphorical thinking is basically regressive and primitive, but when under the control of the ego, it can then serve important adaptive functions. Also related to the adaptive dimension is Klein's (1930) important contribution that symbolization is a necessary ego function of the child for adaptation to other objects from his primary ones, and that accurate symbolization in the internalization of early objects underlies realistic secondary-process thinking. This conceptualization was further extended by another member of the English school, Rycroft (1968), to include the idea that symbolization which leads to adaptive relatedness to new objects is part of the secondary rather than the primary process. Nevertheless, the concept of metaphorical thinking or symbolic expression as regressive has still been kept.

However, from the standpoint of current linguistics and psychological knowledge, the basic assumption in psychoanalytic theory that the development of language historically and individually is from the metaphorical to the conceptual is now open to very serious question. From the vantage point of linguistics (Brown, 1958), there is no hard evidence or data showing any historic linguistic development from the metaphorical to the conceptual. What apparently is present to varying degrees is the observation that the language of an urbanized, industrial-technological society, especially in Western countries, does rely more on conceptual-abstract thinking than metaphorical expression as in a less industrialized society. But this obviously is more a reflection of certain very modern cultural developments in a limited segment of the world, mainly that of Europe and North America, than an inevitable historical development and evolution. Metaphorical thinking is still present to a considerable extent in highly industrialized Japan and other Asian countries. Thus the viewpoint of metaphorical thinking as primitive and archaic may be seen in part as an expression of the nineteenth-century rationalistic philosophies that were so much an outgrowth of the scientific-industrial revolution, earlier based on the Renaissance, Reformation, and Enlightenment, and which so influenced psychoanalytic theorizing. Weber (1920), in a brilliant introduction to *The Protestant Ethic and the Spirit of Capitalism*, traces the development of the rational mode of thought that so characterizes and pervades Western culture. Dumont (1986) is another major contributor to the historical development of rational thought in the culture of Western individualism. From the vantage point of our current understanding from anthropology and area studies of other highly developed non-Western cultures and languages, we can now appreciate that the old attitude of superiority of the scientific *Weltanschauung* of modern Western culture reflects a limited point of view.[2]

On an individual level, it is apparent from the work of Werner (1948) and Piaget (1962) that a child can and does express himself in metaphor. However, a child's use of metaphor is done without any conscious sense of the implications of the metaphor, usually needing an adult to explain the metaphor. This is because children's metaphors often result from incomplete concept-formation, where concept boundaries and categories are still lacking. In other words, from insufficient development of secondary-process thinking. In contrast, the adult's use of the metaphor, whether in artistic, literary, or creative scientific work, is done more consciously and with a fuller view of the implications involved. The adult then uses the metaphor to join disparate elements together in encompassing new and unfamiliar relationships. Thus we believe it is more accurate to state that the adult ability to think in metaphor is a much richer, fuller development of a basic integrative capacity of the ego that is earlier manifested in an incipient form in childhood than the standard psychoanalytic hypothesis that posits all metaphorical thinking as regressive, even when in the service of the ego.[3]

PRIMARY PROCESS AND SYMBOLIZATION

We are now faced with the situation that, if metaphorical thinking, in particular, and the primary process in general, are not well defined by terms such as regressive, archaic, primitive, and inferior, how can this type of thinking be best conceptualized, especially in relation to secondary-process thinking? An important contribution to this problem is the well-conceptualized approach of Noy (1969). His point of view takes off from the emphasis on ego mastery and synthesis, particularly with regard to the self, as developed in the work of Erikson (1968) and George Klein. Noy's main position is that the primary process, in relation to the secondary process, is best defined by function rather than by regression, topography, primitivization, inferiority, or such. The function of primary process is then defined as integrating new experiences into a self-system, as well as giving expression to the self in such areas as dreams and art; while the secondary-process function is in dealing with outer reality, depending on constant feedback. In keeping with the psychoanalytic literature, Noy places all metaphorical thinking as part of the primary process, but posits that the primary process in its imagery develops considerably from childhood to adulthood, as does the secondary process. Relating the two processes to dreams and art, Noy sees the mode of thinking as overwhelmingly primary process in the former, as dreams are given over wholly to expressions of the self. While art is a combination of primary and secondary processes, with emphasis on the primary, as art it is the expression mainly of the self but integrated with gestalt needs for form.

Noy's position is in many respects a well-conceptualized and quite compelling one. Nevertheless, from observations on dreams (see previous chapter) and on art, I believe that a somewhat different formulation from Noy's is necessary. However, before giving evidence from dreams and art for a reformulation, it is important to note how some of the more recent thinking in the related area of symbol-formation and symbolization supports Noy's basic conceptualization of the primary process as related to internalization. This I would like to do in first summarizing the role of symbolization in human development, integrating the work of several writers in the field.

On the basis of the work of such psychologists and psychoanalysts as Werner (1948), Kubie (1958), Angyal (1965), Menaker and Menaker (1965), and Deri (1984), and to a certain extent the English school (Bollas, 1987; Milner, 1987), symbolization and symbolic expression can be conceptualized as a basic capacity and function of the ego, crucial to human development. This conceptualization is also similar to the important philosophical work of Susanne Langer (1942), who stated, "This basic need, which certainly is obvious only in man, is the need for symbolization." I can further formulate from the contributions of these writers that symbolization in its broad sense is related to the basic need of the human being to internalize his environment for development and adaptation; symbolization then serves as a bridge between the inner and outer world. This need to internalize the environment is not only in terms of libidinal development (as Klein emphasizes) and the establishment of object constancy (Hartmann, 1964), but also for the development of various ego functions (as certain writers have emphasized, such as Weiss, 1960; Piaget, 1962; Spitz, 1965; Menaker and Menaker, 1965).[4]

If symbolization is closely related in human development to internalized images in the ego, self and superego, then imagery in dreams, and to a large extent in art, is obviously composed of various internalized images. These may range from body-images (Schilder, 1953) to self-images (Weil, 1958), to identifications and introjects, to identity thema (Lichtenstein, 1977), ego ideals, and various interactions between self and object (Grinker, 1957) with its concomitant self- and object-representations (Jacobson, 1964), to internal objects and self states. Since from earliest life, drive and emotion are experienced in relation to parents and family, and then to their internalizations, intense emotion, conscious or unconscious, is usually related to these internalized images in dreams and in art. Here my conceptualization differs from that of Schafer (1968), who views internalized images as basically devoid of energy and affect.

That dreams are to a large extent composed of various internalized images has been known from the beginning of dream analysis by Freud, and has been emphasized by Kanzer (1955). However, it is my distinct impression that the symbolic expression of various internalized images in art has been insufficiently appreciated, except by some of the English school such as Milner (1957). From my own paintings and etchings, it has quite often been possible to recognize an aesthetic depiction of various identifications and introjects, as well as body and self-images, some from very early childhood. Sometimes such recognition may take months or years after the work of art has been completed. I shall illustrate this in the following chapter.

At this point, I would like to cite my findings from the previous chapter for a reformulation of Noy's position, and to illustrate these findings with a dream below. These comprise observations on dream imagery as related to symbolic expression (metaphorical thinking) and primary process on the one hand, and to paradox and poetic metaphor on the other. I shall briefly restate my observations from the previous chapter.

I find that the primary-process mechanisms of displacement, condensation, and symbolization (in the classical sense) serve a dual function. To the extent that the various mechanisms of the primary process are related to wish-fulfillment, they serve the purpose as stated in the classical psychoanalytic literature of enabling the unconscious wish to evade the superego for expression. Here the primary process is in the service of disguised expression because of the superego, anxiety, and defensive operations. However, when these mechanisms are related to the various psychic structures, to the internalizations of the ego and self, to early object relations, and to dynamics and childhood memories, they serve to give them a rich symbolic expression, depicting just where the psyche is at with regard to various conflicts. Thus the primary process here is in the service of symbolic expression and good symbolic fit, rather than disguise and distortion. It enables the dream to give symbolic expression simultaneously to more diverse aspects of the psyche than any other communication, with the possible exception of art. Thus far, my observations are completely in accord with Noy's formulation of the function of primary process as giving expression to the self.

However, there are two additional observations with regard to poetic metaphor (as differentiated from metaphorical thinking) and paradox in dreams. First, dream imagery has the components to make up poetic metaphors, but never seems to complete the poetic metaphor. A very brief example will illustrate this: in one part of a dream, a man was rehearsing on a thrust stage. He was urged by the directors to sing in a certain way, but decided that his own way would be considerably better. He then asserted himself and sang in his own way. It turned out to be better. Upon close examination of this dream fragment, I found the components of a poetic metaphor: the concrete image and symbol of the thrust stage and the more abstract image of self-assertion in singing his own way. The poetic metaphor would be: "on the thrust stage of his manhood." But the metaphor is obviously not completed in the dream.

With regard to imagery and paradox in dreams, I have found that, after I am successfully able to analyze a dream in relation to its relevant context, that is, upon closer scrutiny of the total dream in its multifaceted symbolic expression, the latent content falls into two basic structural elements (in terms of structural linguistics)[5] of seeming opposites or contradictions. In other words, after the associations are obtained, and after the knowledge of primary-process mechanisms is utilized, interpretations always seem to integrate opposites into statements effectively explaining the relevant context. Thus dreams have the makings of effective paradoxes, where contradictory lines of thought are synthesized into a fuller truth. But here I must emphasize, as with poetic metaphor, that dreams do not complete the paradox. This integration into a fuller truth must be done by the creative act of interpretation.

These observations lead me to conclude that there is a hierarchical organization of expression in dreams: from the disguised expression of wishes to a multifaceted symbolic expression of diverse aspects and processes of the psyche, to incomplete poetic metaphors, to structural opposites in the latent content as incipient paradoxes. It is thus apparent that primary-process mechanisms do not occur haphazardly in dreams but are used in the service of hierarchical modes of direct as well as indirect expression. These conclusions are in keeping with Ehren-zweig's (1967) theory of a hidden organization in primary process in art. However, I must further conclude that while primary-process mechanisms and symbolic expression (metaphorical thinking) go hand in hand in the dream in giving a rich expression to the psyche, poetic metaphor and paradox must be completed by the more conscious efforts of analyst and analyzand in the integrative process of interpreta-tion.[6] Experience reveals that there is real value in psychoanalytic therapy in the interpretive integration of structural opposites, but very little, if any, value in forming poetic metaphors from the dream.

A DREAM AS SYMBOLIC EXPRESSION

An examination of a dream in detail is now in order to illustrate these hierarchical modes of expression; the relationship of primary-process mechanisms to wish-fulfillment and multifaceted symbolic expression, incomplete poetic metaphor and structural opposites in the latent content as incipient paradoxes. The dream I shall present is the same as in the last chapter. However, while some of its analysis is obviously the same, the emphasis in this chapter will be more on modes of expression than interpretive use of the dream in clinical work. The dream was that of a 21-year-old girl, Jane, who had been in psychoanalytic therapy for one and a half years after coming to New York City from Boston. The transference was still one of a strong over-idealization of the therapist, who was thus looked upon as a friendly ally. Not until over a year after the dream was reported did the intense negative transferences develop in a transference neurosis. The relevant context of the dream was her bringing her boyfriend, Charles, home to her parents and brother for the first time, with a considerable reaction of little understood anxiety that the visit home would somehow completely sabotage her current good relationship with Charles. The dream was reported after a stage in therapy of working on her pervasive reaction of apathy when visiting home. It had become apparent and was interpreted to her that she was caught in a conflict between strong dependency needs on her parents on the one hand, and their striking inability to allow any striving on her part towards autonomy and individualization without their cutting off their relationship with her, on the other. These interpretations enabled her to become somewhat more self-assertive and less apathetic in striving towards her own identity.

Jane's dream (restated)

I am driving in a section of North Boston. It's full of violence and I'm afraid. I'm following my brother in his car [a sports car], but not too closely. I don't want him to know I'm following him. [On later inquiry, she associated that she was afraid to follow him too closely in childhood, as he didn't want her tagging after him.] I'm hoping he'll lead the way out. Then, I remember I'm to meet Charles at the train station and I'm afraid I'll be late and miss the train and him.

Upon further questioning her for a fuller description of the dream scene, she gradually recognized that the surroundings were very similar to the neighborhood she grew up in as a young child, another section of Boston. She then spontaneously associated that North Boston is in reality an African-American neighborhood in contrast to the area she had lived in. She further described the people on the streets as being silently and sullenly violent, with much pent-up rage.

I shall first use the dream to explicate the relationship of primary process to wish-fulfillment on the one hand, and symbolic expression on the other. It is apparent that in one use, primary-process displacement operates through the image of the silently and sullenly violent blacks to give disguised expression and fulfillment to Jane's feelings of rage. However, from the standpoint of symbolic expression, this displacement also represents accurately the defensive operations of the ego, showing that by ego-distancing (Sheppard and Saul, 1958) she is mainly out of touch with or has repressed her inner feelings of rage. Moreover, the fact that her rage is represented by many others rather than by one indicates its intensity; and her reaction of fear to the blacks also shows her anxiety over the repressed rage becoming expressed. We further find that through condensation, the image of the silently and sullenly violent blacks with much pent-up rage not only aids in the disguised expression of the rage, but also gives excellent representation or symbolic expression of the nature of her reaction to rigidly enforced compliance by her parents, of her masochistic self-image of being the subservient underdog at home, and of her repressed feelings threatening current good object relationships. Another example of this dual use of primary process is when she follows the brother's car, which is leading the way out. Here, through the symbol of the car (in the classic psychoanalytic sense), there is disguised expression of phallic strivings and penis envy. But also given symbolic expression is the brother as ego ideal, an ideal of actual rebellion in the family that might represent a way out from enforced compliance with its resultant destructive rage. Further represented through her associations is her fear of following too closely in his footsteps, that is, the fear of being the rebellious girl and of giving expression to her phallic urges.

With regard to incomplete metaphors, several are present in the dream. The images of the silently and sullenly violent people as blacks in her childhood neighborhood obviously represent through displacement and ego-distancing her own repressed ego state from childhood. Blackness, rage, and a childhood ego state are components of a metaphor that is really not completed in the dream. Resolved, the poetic metaphor would read, "the blackness of my childhood rage." In the image of following her brother's car, which she hopes will lead the way out, elements of another incomplete metaphor are present. As we noted above, the brother was associated with the rebellious one in the family in contrast to her own subservience. Thus rebellion, following him, and hoping he'll lead the way out become elements for an incomplete poetic metaphor. Here the completed metaphor would be "rebelling in my brother's footsteps as a way out." The final metaphor in the dream incorporates missing the train associated with the breaking up of her love relationship with Charles. Here, the metaphor would be constituted as "missing the boat [train] in my love relationship."

With regard to the structural opposites in the latent content, let me first summarize the dream as a multifaceted symbolic expression from our work on it above. In the first part, great anxiety was depicted over intense feelings of repressed rage (the silent and sullenly violent blacks with pent-up rage) from childhood (the old neighborhood). Also depicted through the blacks is a passive, subservient childhood adaptation with a self-image of the victim. In the next part of the dream, there is a fearful wish of following the brother's example at home of open rebellion as a way out of her subservience and repressed rage, through the expression of phallic urges (following his car). Penis envy of the brother is also present. Finally, there is the fear of missed communication and a breaking up of the relationship with Charles (missing Charles's train – Kanzer, 1955). The structural opposites in the latent content are the repressed rage of childhood, and its fearful expression, from a subservient, masochistic adaptation at home on the one hand; and, on the other, the fear of the breaking up of a love relationship with Charles. Putting it in a more literary mode of expression, rage and love are juxtaposed, and form the elements of a possible paradox that must clarify the anxiety expressed in the relevant context.

Before delineating how the structural opposites were integrated in clarifying the relevant context, it is important to note that intrapsychic conflict as depicted in the dream does not really coincide with the structural opposites. For conflict in this dream revolves around a masochistic, subservient adaptation from childhood with considerable repressed rage, as against more open self-assertive and rebellious behavior. The conflict is dynamically prolonged because of internalized images of the parents cutting off their love relationship with her if there was any self-assertion on her part. Further conflict concerns the possible breaking through of the rage to actual manifestation. The interpretive work pointed out to Jane that she was afraid that her visit home with Charles would reestablish the old forms of masochistic relationship with her parents in the context of some newly won self-assertion. This in turn would reevoke intense responses of rage from childhood, with considerable anxiety that the rage might spill over into her relationship with Charles, thus wrecking it. Further, that the one way out she could now visualize in the dream was to follow in her brother's footsteps by being more openly rebellious at home.

I have now noted the hierarchical modes of expression in dreams and have illustrated them with a dream example. At this point, we may question how our findings in dreams relate to art. First, in both dreams and art, primary-process mechanisms and symbolic expression or metaphorical thinking are clearly in evidence (Ehrenzweig, 1967; Noy, 1968). Second, works of art are composed in various ways of poetic metaphors, and usually reach a final paradoxical integration (Brooks, 1960), whereas, as we have seen in dreams, poetic metaphors are incomplete and structural opposites in the latent content are not yet integrated into paradox. Thus the creative process in art is present in dreams in only an incipient stage, and needs the later creative work of analyzand and analyst with associations and interpretations to do the necessary integrations. In another comparison, paradox and metaphor in both dreams and art only gain meaning in relation to context. In dreams, the structural opposites of the latent content can only be effectively integrated in interpretation in relation to the relevant context in a patient's life situation or therapy as I have discussed in the previous chapter. In art, metaphor and paradox gain meaning in relation to the context of the work in which they appear.[7]

PRIMARY AND SECONDARY PROCESS IN ART

Since poetic metaphor and paradox are integral parts of art, and are manifested in incipient stages in dreams, the next problem is conceptualizing their relationship to primary- and secondary-process thinking. There are several different possibilities for conceptualizing this relationship. The first possibility is extending the definition of primary process to include poetic metaphor and paradox, as well as metaphorical thinking. This has been Noy's (1968, 1969) choice, and in his theory everything that is integrative and expressive of the self is considered part of the primary process. However, my finding that poetic metaphor and paradox are manifested in only an incipient stage in dreams, and need later conscious creative integrative work, seems to make this approach invalid. A second possibility is that of Arieti's (1967) positing a tertiary process which integrates both primary and secondary processes in art and other forms of creativity. A third approach is in locating the particular creative integrations manifested in poetic metaphor and paradox in a more refined or developed part of the secondary process. This third conceptualization is a more economic one than Arieti's creation of a totally new tertiary process. This conceptualization is supported by Rothenberg's (1979) finding that highly creative writers tend to be constantly thinking in and integrating seemingly contra-dictory lines of thought and feelings into new syntheses. Moreover, a different conceptualization from Arieti, as well as from Kris (1952), is needed of the relationship of primary- to secondary-process thinking in the arts. It is developed below. My approach is also related to the theory of ego functioning as developed by Menaker and Menaker (1965): that the ego is not simply involved in mastery and synthesis, but strives for new levels of integration in psychosocial evolution. Thus poetic metaphor, paradox, analytic interpretive integrations, and creative scientific insights as well, are all in the service of an ego striving towards new integrations, and seeking new relationships.

At this point, we are still left with the problem of the relationship of the primary process to the secondary process in art. From the conceptualization of poetic metaphor and paradox as highly imaginative aspects of the secondary process, I would see art as governed in a hierarchical manner by this highly developed part of the secondary process, with symbolic expression (metaphorical thinking) and the mechanisms of the primary process in descending order being subservient to this part of the secondary process.[8] This contrasts with creative scientific work where we suspect this highly imaginative integrative part of the secondary process works with and governs more logical conceptual parts of the secondary process, with relatively little if any manifestation of the primary process. I further view these hierarchical modes of functioning in art as relatively unitary cognitive modes of functioning. This is in contrast to Kris who postulated alternating states between secondary and primary process functioning in art. My own experience in art, confirmed by other artists, indicates that except for later revision of the work, there is a relatively stable, unitary cognitive mode, and ego state of functioning, which I would submit combines aspects of the secondary and primary process in a hierarchical manner.

At this point, we may inquire briefly into the relationship of primary- and secondary-process thinking in dreams and art with preconscious mentation, particularly as explicated by Kubie (1958, 1978). It is apparent that preconscious mentation is present in both dreams and art in the form of metaphorical expression, and in art in the forms of paradox and poetic metaphor. However, while Kubie concentrates on the presence of preconscious processes in different areas of psychic functioning, the emphasis here can be viewed as differentiating the nature of preconscious mentation in dreams and art, with implications for other areas of psychic functioning as well. This is done through explicating the varying relationships of primary- to different aspects of secondary-process thinking in unitary cognitive modes of a hierarchical nature.

My conclusions point to an area for further research. They imply and suggest that we further develop concepts of different cognitive modes. These modes would be according to the particular combinations of primary- and secondary-process thinking in the variety of functions (such as art and scientific work) in which we direct our mind. This would also have to take into account different aspects of the secondary process itself (differentiating logical-conceptual from poetic-paradoxical or integrative-intuitive) in these various combinations. This position is in general accord with Langer's work (1953) on different kinds of symbolization serving both art and science. This viewpoint is also supported by my self-observations in a variety of different pursuits that I operate in significantly different cognitive modes and ego states in writing a scientific paper, doing psychoanalytic therapy with patients, painting and etching, and working on plays and librettos. In this I find that significantly different cognitive modes are not only present between art and scientific work and psychoanalytic therapy, but also between different art forms as well, such as painting and playwriting. I must conclude by admitting that here we are now only beginning to grapple with the basic problems in this whole area.

NOTES

1. Here it is important to differentiate metaphorical thinking in its popular usage from poetic metaphor. The former is characterized by a general substitution or representation of one mode of thought by another, usually through some type of figure of speech or analogy. Various facets of the psyche can be expressed metaphorically. Poetic metaphor, on the other hand, is characterized by a joining together of different levels of experience, often concrete and abstract, to establish new relationships to convey social and universal meanings. I am indebted to Professor Gino Rizzo for this clarification. In this chapter I shall use metaphorical thinking interchangeably with symbolic expression. I mean by these terms a more inclusive representation of all aspects of the psyche than the classical psychoanalytic use of symbols, which are substitute representations of the id only. Symbolic expression is inclusive of the psychoanalytic symbol, but is not limited to it.
2. See Erikson (1969) for an excellent explication of one non-Western culture's way of thinking and Roland's (1988, 1996) more comprehensive consideration of the culture/psychology of Indians and Japanese as compared to Euro-Americans.
3. I am indebted to Nancy Dorian, formerly Professor of Linguistics at Bryn Mawr College, and Albert Rothenberg, formerly Director of Research, Austen Riggs, for clarification of these points.
4. This raises the whole issue of how to conceptualize the close interrelationship of ego function and internalization, which still remains a strong controversy in the psychoanalytic field. Historically, Freud (1923b) treated the ego both in terms of function and internalization (identifications). Hartmann (1964), in a paper in the

1930s, called for a separation of function and internalization, relegating function to the ego and internalization to the self. Most, though by no means all, contemporary psychoanalytic ego psychologists follow Hartmann's division. My own preference is to keep Freud's formulation of viewing the ego in the paradoxical or bimodal manner of both function and internalization. The rationale for this conceptual preference is that evidence is present (Klein, 1930; Menaker and Menaker, 1965; Spitz, 1965, and Weiss, 1960) that internalization and function are inextricably interwoven from earliest infancy; that is, that the most basic ego functions such as reality-testing, depend on proper internalization. Further, it is now clear that imitation, egotization, and identification play important roles in the development of most ego functions in childhood. By keeping this dual formulation of the ego, theoretical attention is kept more focused on the crucial interrelationship of function and internalization. Hartmann did not seem to be sufficiently aware in his writings of this close interrelationship. As a result, though his conceptualization is obviously a workable one, it is probably no accident that most of the ego psychologists following his theorizing have paid insufficient attention to the effect of internalization on function in both normal and psychopathological development, as well as on transferences.

5. In structural linguistics, oppositions or balancing factors are found to be intrinsic to the very structure of all languages.

6. This is not to preclude those rare dreams of creative discovery, which Freud noted and assigned to the prior work of the preconscious, later incorporated into the dream.

7. Many of these aspects of the relationship between art and dreams emerged in conversations with Albert Rothenberg.

8. Noy (1968) and Ehrenzweig (1967) also see art in a hierarchical combination of secondary and primary processes, but with the secondary process mainly constituting principles of aesthetic form. This is in contrast to the thesis of my argument in this chapter, that poetic metaphor and paradox as the crux of creative work in art are part of the secondary process. This is in addition to considerations of principles of aesthetic form, which we also view as being part of the secondary process, but as being subordinate to the central organization, or integration of opposites, in the work of art, as well as conveying important meanings.

5

Imagery and the Self in Artistic Creativity

ARTIST'S USE OF IMAGERY

The artist's imagery provides one of the essential bases on which his creativity rests. His use of imagery cuts two ways: on the one hand, the poet is able to formulate new integrations and meanings through the use of poetic metaphor, paradox, and other structures; on the other, he is able to draw upon his own unconscious and express it metaphorically. Images can thus be likened to a ladder that reaches up into the artist's imagination and down into his unconscious. Or perhaps the artist's use of imagery is like a signpost at a crossroads: on the same post are arrows pointing in the direction of varied social and universal meanings, and others pointing down the road of individual psychobiography or of various unconscious meanings. Neither of these similes, however, conveys the relationship of the unconscious meanings of imagery to the more universal ones at the core of the artistic endeavor. And however one analogizes this process, it is incumbent upon the psychoanalytic critic to synthesize these two uses of imagery in any given work. To the extent that he ignores this problem, more often than not he proceeds into the dead end of reductionism, the bane of psychoanalytic literary criticism.

I should make clear at once that imagery is obviously not the only vehicle the artist uses in his work. There are many other formal and structural elements that are crucial to artists' conveying their particular viewpoint or meanings. Such elements must also be taken into account by the psychoanalytic critic. In this chapter, however, I shall concentrate on the artist's use of imagery because it so crucially relates to the use of the primary process in creativity, with highly relevant implications for psychoanalytic criticism.

To effect a valid integration of the two uses of imagery, it is important to assess the prevailing theory of creativity in psychoanalysis by such major writers as Ernst Kris (1952), Anton Ehrenzweig (1967), and Pincus Noy (1968). These writers in various ways all locate the main cognitive thrust of the creative process in the primary process with its richly overdetermined, emotionally charged, imagistic thinking. The products of the primary process are then integrated with and governed by secondary-process considerations of aesthetic form and structure. The way each of these writers formulates this varies, but there is a basic congruency of viewpoint among them. In effect, they have worked out in a far more sophisticated way Freud's (1906) original thesis that the work of art consists of a daydream dressed in aesthetic clothes.

This accepted framework of the cognitive processes of creativity is questioned by the work of Albert Rothenberg (1979), a psycho-analytically oriented psychiatrist, on the creative process. His meth-odology relies neither on the couch nor simply on evaluating the literary text, but rather on systematic interviews with outstanding creative writers in the actual process of creation. He has found that some of the main cognitive processes of creativity involve what he has termed janusian and homospatial thinking. The former is the meaning-ful integration of antithetical elements, while the latter incorporates different, discrete elements simultaneously, essential to the formation of metaphor. Most crucial is the fact that these types of cognition cannot be located within the primary process, but are an imaginative part of the secondary process, or what Rothenberg terms translogical thinking. In partial support of his viewpoint, I have found that paradox and poetic metaphor are present in only incipient forms in dreams. Moreover, Rothenberg has been able to confirm the presence of janusian and homospatial thinking in outstanding creative scientists as well as writers.

Rothenberg's work thus challenges the prevailing views on creativity in psychoanalysis and raises major questions. If the cognitive processes of creativity are primarily located within a refined or imaginative part of the secondary process, then to what extent, if at all, does the primary process enter into creativity? And, if it is involved in the creative process, in what way?

PRIMARY PROCESS AND CREATIVITY

First, a personal observation that furnishes a possible answer to these questions. Some years ago, I was very much struck with an old maple tree in the vicinity of our country house; so much so I decided to do an etching of it. Much of the maple was dead, but new shoots were also coming up. As I rendered this image in an etching, these oppositions of deadness and new life became integrated in an artistically valid way. Some time later, it became apparent to me from the nature of the peeling bark and such that the textures of the old maple related metaphorically to an early unconscious body-image of a severe burn I had suffered as a very young child. Thus, a very deep personal element from the primary process entered into a broader metaphor incorporating the oppositions of deadness and life. I may add parenthetically that over the years some artistically gifted patients have strongly related to this etching which hangs in my office, considering it as a metaphor for the therapeutic process: new life and growth emerging from devastation. My conclusion is that individual metaphorical elements, even on an unconscious level, enter into poetic metaphor and its broader social meanings, lending a strong emotional undertone and communicative power to the work of art.

This conclusion of course derives from observation of my own artistic work, though supported by a number of other examples in addition to the one just cited. Can it be confirmed by other data? I shall first turn to a painting done immediately after the World Trade Center attack by a patient, Flora, a nationally recognized artist. She had viewed the whole scenario – the planes crashing into the World Trade Center and the buildings burning and collapsing – from her studio window just several blocks north. In a semi-abstract mode, she painted the vertical steel beams of the World Trade Center across a large canvas. Some time after the painting was finished, she realized that the vertical steel beams also looked like the slats of a picket fence that surrounded the house where she had grown up. It was in a tropical country where houses are elevated far off the ground with the picket fence enclosing the space under the house. It was an important imaginative space for her as a child where she would spend hours drawing. But it was also a space where a sadistic, and sometimes violent, brother would come to harass her. Thus, the imagery she consciously used as a metaphor to depict a current-day devastation and trauma simultaneously unconsciously expressed metaphorically both her strongly maintaining her artistic identity in the midst of it, and the childhood emotional trauma of attacks by her brother. The latter meanings thus lent a more powerful emotional tone to the painting.

Let me now turn to an example from poetry. It is extremely rare to have access to such data related to the actual act of creating. Fortunately, in Rothenberg's paper (1976), "Homospatial thinking in creativity," an example is given in detail of the formation of a poem that is relevant to my purposes. I shall cite portions of his paper to give evidence how the writer uses primary-process material, or the personally metaphorical, to reinforce and give impact to his more abstract meanings.

A major poet formulates initial ideas for a poem several months after a visit to the Southwest and an unusual experience of retreating to his car during a windstorm and seeing a bedraggled horse suddenly appearing from out of nowhere.

> Hot pumice blew
> Through Monument Valley
> The Elephant rock ached
> The Three Sisters wailed
> It was not the place for a picnic
> We ate in the car's shade
> Hunched over at top speed
> Looking up, there was our guest, our ghost
> At death's door
> Slender, tottering liquid eyed ...

Then the poet reports having two dreams, dreamt the night after he had formulated these initial lines. The dreams are as follows.

Dream one

J. T. [pseudonym initials of the poet's male friend] and I are on a trip or a visit. We come to a soccer field and feel like playing, even though one must pay to do so. If we start at once, we shall have two hours worth for a few dollars apiece. But the other players delay. Next, indoors, we are shown a room with two daybeds. Miriam enters and begins compulsively to make up my bed, rather to tear it apart under the guise of making it. I keep asking her not to, and finally am angry. She falls back in a swoon dressed only in underclothes. Other people enter slowly: J. T. in a sweatshirt and a boring old couple I am stuck with throughout the party. I have made my own bed by then.

Dream two

I've taken a position in a large comfortable house. I am to be the companion of a very old woman – at least 100. After many preliminaries I am led (by my mother among others, but we treat each other like polite strangers) through halls and up stairs to arrive at the invalid's apartments. I expect her to be bedridden but in honor of the occasion she has risen to meet me at the door, an ancient dwarf with my grandmother's face, head smiling and enlarged, in a blue dress. My mother, with a practiced movement, takes the old creature onto her shoulders. I touch her hands. They are horribly small, a baby's – no, hands made by a plastic surgeon, the last joints missing from the fingers, and little false nails attached. We sit down to supper – she in her chair, I on the end of a chaise-longue. Her teeth have little secondary fangs attached, which enable her to eat. People are watching. It is clear we are going to be delighted with each other. In an old unused electric heater is mounted a bad copy of a portrait, coarsely colored and printed, of R. G. [pseudonym initials of an old family friend]. There's some question of destroying it.

The poet reports to the interviewer the thought behind the poem, "horses live human lives," i.e. "that horses, while they were beasts and clearly nonhuman were, at the same time, members of the human species," is clearly a janusian expression of opposites. The poet then added to his initial lines the phrase, "A tradition in China as in modern verse / Gives to each age its emblematic beast ... the horse, in its nature of both beast and nonbeast, human and nonhuman, simultaneously, would be the emblem of our times, the emblem of the currently ubiquitous and much-discussed dilemma of alienation."

Several days later, he wrote the final poem: In Monument Valley.

One spring twilight, during a lull in the war,
At Shoup's farm south of Troy, I last rode horseback.
Stillnesses were swarming inward from the evening star
Or outward from the buoyant sorrel mare

Who moved as if not displeased by the weight upon her.
Meadows received us, heady with unseen lilac.
Brief, polyphonic lives abounded everywhere.
With one accord we circled the small lake.

Yet here I set among the crazy shapes things take.
Wasp-waisted to a fault by long abrasion,
The "Three Sisters" howl, "Hell's Gate" yawns wide.
I'm eating something in the cool Hertz car

When the shadow falls. There has come to my door
As to death's this creature stunted, cinder-eyed,
Tottering still half in trust, half in fear of man –
Dear god, a horse. I offer my apple-core

But she is past hunger, she lets it roll in the sand,
And I, I raise the window and drive on.
About the ancient bond between her kind and mine
Little more to speak of can be done.

It is apparent upon examination that while the poem is considerably
different from the initial lines, the last three stanzas dealing with his
experience in Monument Valley are directly related to both those initial
lines and to the janusian thoughts about horses expressed to the
interviewer. In effect, these last three stanzas were conceived and
written first. What about the first two stanzas?

On the morning after the dreams, the poet returned to working on
the poem, and "dimly conceived in his mind's eye an image of the horse
and rider and of the horse alone, all occupying the same space" – an
example of homospatial thinking. He then conceived of the following
lines related to the homospatial image, and put them at the end of his
initial lines. "A gentle broken horse / For all he knew it could have been
I who first / Broke him, rode him, abandoned him / When I went off to
study or to war."

The following day he decided to emphasize the past relationship
between horse and rider, to bring them together right away, and shift
the idea to the beginning of the poem. The lines became as follows:
"We live mostly in the past or in the future / These lines begin in one
and end in the other / It was the first or second summer after the war /
That I last found myself on horseback."

These lines then became the basis for the first two stanzas. Thus, the
homospatial conception enabled the poet to render a strong sense of
unity between human and animal in the beginning contacting sharply
with the alienation and separation at the end, the change strongly
suggested by allusions to war.

We are now at a point where I can begin raising the question of what role the dreams, or primary-process thinking, played in the creation of this poem. First, in approaching the meaning of dreams, one must first ask the context of any particular dream, or what the dream is related to in a person's life. I think it apparent that, since the poet had just started working on the poem, these two dreams are clearly related to the poem. The poet before dreaming had already formulated the last three stanzas dealing with poignant and devastating alienation and separation in our times. But he needed to complete the first part of the poem. Second, I now assume that the primary process not only gives disguised expression to forbidden wishes in dreams, but also excellent metaphorical depiction of various aspects of the self and early object relations – a point of view developed independently by Pincus Noy (1969) and Susan Deri (1984), and incorporated into my own work on dreams.

Two dreams in the same night are as we know intrinsically related. The first dream seems to deal with peers, though it appears there is a rejection of sexuality out of strong needs for autonomy and individuation. "I go my own way" is later associated to the dream thought, "I have made my own bed by then." Having opted for individuation in the present, the poet seems to allow himself unconsciously to go into the primeval, intense relationship with mother and grandmother in the second dream. The imagery and associations not only imply Oedipal wishes, but also the old symbiotic modes of relating, which are pictured as both satisfying and burdensome.

It is interesting to note that the mare (mother) carrying the rider in the first two stanzas is related to the dream imagery of the mother carrying the grandmother on her back. Even more significant is the fact that, after the dreams and the homospatial conception, the poet changed the sex of the horse from a stallion to a mare – afterwards being cognizant of the fact that mare in French is "mother" ("mère") in the way it sounds.

The poet, after formulating the homospatial image of horse and rider and horse alone, then added lines on after the first ones already completed, that strongly convey the relationship of man to horse and to himself as one of union (breaking in and riding) and abandonment, just the conflicts of the self portrayed in the first two dreams. He then rejects such an explicit formulation of this conflict, making it far more implicit in the new lines, and shifting these lines to the beginning of the poem where it can contrast with the later alienation. In a further and final revision, the poet keeps only the union of man and horse, which so contrasts to the last three stanzas, and which only anticipate them by "the lull in the war" and "Troy."

My conclusion is that these dreams served for the poet the function of putting him in touch with certain aspects of his self and early relationships that were crucial to draw upon to complete the poem. In effect, the poet drew upon the primary process for powerful affective feelings and relationships relating to Oedipal and PreOedipal symbiotic ties to his mother and grandmother to fuel the more abstract ideas of unity needed at the beginning of the poem. The closeness of man and horse in the first two stanzas is poetically moving and affectively powerful. The imagery of the horse as mare then touches upon the personal as well as serving as a poetic metaphor for a former social unity.

I believe this analysis of the poet's use of the primary process in his dreams in the act of creating accords well with my own self-observations on the creation of an etching and with Flora's painting of the World Trade Center. It also touches on Holland's important hypothesis in psychoanalytic criticism that unconscious, childhood emotional fantasies fuel all arts. My own approach differs from him in two important respects, both illustrated in the next chapter: (a) the fantasy may involve important aspects of the self and early object relations, as well as the psychosexual that Holland at that time so exclusively emphasized; and (b) the search of psychoanalytic criticism is not simply to arrive at the presence of these fantasies, but rather to see how these fantasies support the more universal and abstract meanings of the work. Thus, the personal elements support the more abstract poetic metaphors and paradoxes, which convey more social and universal meanings.

IMAGERY AND DEFENSES

Having established my point, that the artist is able to use the personal in service of the more universal meanings of metaphor, further questions may be raised as to whether the artist is truly more in touch with himself than most persons are, and to what extent the process of artistic creation brings about personal change in the artist. Often the former point is raised in the form, "did the artist really know what he was communicating, or are we just reading this into his work?" Both questions are more complex than they seem at first glance.

Much of the answer to both questions lies, I believe, in the very nature and use of imagery. *Imagery bypasses defenses*. Thus, when artists use imagery as a major aesthetic means of conveying abstract, social meanings reinforced by the personal meanings, they by and large bypass their own defensive structure. Imagery is therefore a window to the unconscious, even when used for aesthetic purposes. In dreams, for example, although defensive processes are often present, the imagery and its underlying meanings – via associations and primary-process mechanisms – usually convey many more unconscious aspects of the psyche than in waking-life communications. Again, I believe, because imagery bypasses defenses. Through this use of imagery, the artist has, as it were, a direct tap on his or her unconscious. But, and I must qualify this as an important "but," the unconscious is essentially used for the artistic endeavor and not for increased self-awareness, as in psychoanalysis.

Returning for a moment to my initial example of the etching of the Old Maple, I was not at the time that much in touch with my childhood body-image, nor did my awareness of it become enhanced after doing the etching. It was only later in the psychoanalytic process that I became conscious of this body-image, and only then could relate it to this etching. Time and again I have found the same to be true of this process in other works of mine. On the other hand, there is the other example I have used of the poem, where the poet to some extent became aware that the first part of the poem included his mother. As a psychoanalyst, I would not, however, consider this to be a very major step in increased self-awareness. In conclusion, I would hypothesize that because imagery bypasses defenses, the artist far more than others is able to tap his or her own unconscious, but essentially in the service of the artistic endeavor, and usually without any significant increase in self-awareness.

By the same token, since the defensive structure is circumvented, little is basically changed in terms of the artist's unconscious conflicts. For a cardinal point of psychoanalysis posits that the analysis of resistance and the defensive structure of a patient is a sine qua non for basic therapeutic change. If the defensive structure remains untouched, as it is in artistic creation, then the unconscious conflicts remain basically unaltered. This accords with the observation that an artist may be extremely self-expressive, but still remain quite emotionally disturbed.

CREATIVITY, IDENTITY, AND THE COLLECTIVE

Does this mean, however, that artistic creation has little or no effect on the artist's personality? Psychoanalysts such as Otto Rank (1932) and much later, Margaret Brenman-Gibson (1981), posit a profound relationship between changes in the artist and artistic creativity. But to understand these changes, I must shift ground psychoanalytically from the dimensions I have so far used in this chapter of topography, that is, conscious and preconscious versus unconscious, and primary-process versus secondary-process thinking, to a psychology of the self and identity. Both Rank and Brenman-Gibson posit that the artist struggles with a transformation or reintegration of the artist's self or various identity elements which the collectivity or audience is also simultaneously and inarticulately struggling with, as a pre-condition for artistic creativity. Further, they maintain that the very act of artistic creation helps the artist in this new identity integration, as well as articulating the audience's own struggles and helping them towards new integrations, thus gaining for the artist social recognition or mirroring of the new identity integrations in himself. Thus, profound changes may indeed take place in the artist, but more by way of integrating various warring identity elements tied in to the sociohistorical reality of his times than from resolving certain unconscious conflicts stemming from childhood, although these two are obviously interrelated.

Brenman-Gibson (1981) in her book, *Clifford Odets: American Playwright* shows how Clifford Odets transformed many of his own warring-identity elements through his tremendously popular plays in the 1930s, while touching on many similar themes in the American audiences of that era. My own psychoanalytic experience with an Indian writer confirms this point of view. His own identity struggles as a member of the upper-middle-class, urban, educated elite who became totally alienated from Hindu culture, are in good part expressed and partially resolved through his writings, while articulating for many members of the Indian intelligentsia their own profound struggles with Westernization. It became apparent that his inner struggles to resolve these warring identity elements both preceded his writing, and were in good part aided by the very act of writing. Certain conflicts still remained quite unconscious and unaffected by his writing, but there is no question that through his creative work he had fashioned a far more meaningful adult identity integration than before, one relevant to contemporary Indians struggling to assert the validity of their own identity and culture.

PART III

Psychoanalytic Criticism

6

Toward a Reorientation of Psychoanalytic Literary Criticism

INTRODUCTION

"It's a devastation!" Lionel Trilling, one of the first of the critics to use psychoanalysis, averred in his last years about psychoanalytic criticism (personal communication). Another, Leon Edel (1969), so despaired over the misuse of psychoanalysis in literary criticism because of conflicting approaches to symbolic expression, that he strongly urged psychoanalysis to be confined to biography only. Frederick Crews (1976) ran up the red flag over intrinsic, reductionistic tendencies in psychoanalytic criticism, warning that only the utmost caution can prevent the ubiquitous misuse of psychoanalysis. And yet we are paradoxically faced with a swelling movement by literary critics as well as psychoanalysts to use psychoanalysis in criticism.

Is psychoanalytic literary criticism, then, simply a popular cul-de-sac? Or is psychoanalysis, rather a viewpoint pertinent to literary understanding, but one fraught with danger from hidden problems just beneath the surface of easy synthesis? If we are to speak of psychoanalytic literary criticism, rather than simply applied psychoanalysis, where one may romp freely without regard for the ecology of another discipline, then we must talk in the dialogue of a serious interdisciplinary effort. And such interdisciplinary explorations invariably lead into uncharted areas.

In particular, the psychoanalytic critic has a most difficult time in negotiating the straits between psychological reductionism and ignorance of the complexities of either psychoanalysis or aesthetics. The monster of psychological reductionism usually fells the critic through his reliance on an essentializing strategy (Burke, 1941b) of reducing all motivation and content to the psychological or to infantile conflicts (Crews, 1976) or by his unquestioning acceptance of the basic

assumptions of traditional applied psychoanalysis, assumptions that I
hope to show reduce the literary work to a psychological framework,
rather than expand the dimensions of the aesthetic experience. If this
many-headed monster has not laid the critic low, then more often than
not another sweeps into its vortex of ignorance the psychoanalyst
unfamiliar with the basics of aesthetics as well as the literary critic
friendly to psychoanalysis but unaware of its theoretical and historical
complexities. Even when the analyst-reader has some substantial
grounding in criticism and the critic has taken psychoanalytic courses,
there still remains the problem of not having acquired the sophistication
and discrimination that comes from working in a field over many years.
Such deficiencies, of course, are common to any interdisciplinary
undertaking.

How, then, can some of the riches already attained in psychoanalytic
literary criticism, and even applied psychoanalysis, be accounted for if
the picture I have painted is so truly bleak? Ironically, the literary critic
and psychoanalyst are remarkably similar in that their individual
sensitivities, insights, and imagination often transcend their theoretical
orientation in determining the validity of their work. Talent and flair
often tend to prevail over methodology in these two fields. It is from
just these individual gifts of perceptiveness and imagination that I
suspect that much of the promise of psychoanalytic literary criticism has
been realized. Are we then to chuck overboard all theoretical
considerations, relying simply on raw intuition? Obviously not. No
one would gainsay the need for a sound theoretical framework.

It is just to this need for a guide for better integration, rather than a
new aesthetic, that I would like to address this paper. As a psychoanalyst
with some grounding in literary criticism, I am under no illusion of the
potentially perilous territory I shall be exploring, and rather expect that
I too on occasion shall run up on the shoals. My confidence of some
success, however, is predicated on my own work differentiating art
from the dream (see Chapter 4), experience in interdisciplinary
collaboration on drama criticism, and familiarity with other very recent
explorations into the creative process and primary-process thinking that
are fraught with important implications for integrating psychoanalysis
with literary criticism.

Before embarking in a new direction, discretion indicates a rather
careful examination of old pitfalls that have led so many astray. In
particular, I shall demonstrate, at times ad nauseum, how so much of

psychoanalytic literary criticism and applied psychoanalysis is based on a certain analogy of the work of art with the dream and daydream, an analogy that must be seriously challenged because it interferes with valid criticism by invariably pointing the critic toward reducing art to a psychological framework. I see this as the fundamental cause of reductionism, one that leads the psychoanalytic critic down the garden path of invariably searching for infantile conflicts and latent content. In broad outline, I shall chart how this basic analogy has influenced almost the entire field of psychoanalytic literary criticism, and how in recent decades this analogy has been greatly reinforced by very facilely attractive formulations on the creative process that have lured the critic astray and wrecked his efforts. These formulations too are now open to serious question.

In the second part of this chapter, I shall consider how literary critics have been influenced by psychoanalysis, and especially by the basic assumptions and analogy just cited as they influence the development of a new aesthetic by such critics as Simon O. Lesser (1957), Frederick Hoffman (1957), and Norman Holland (1964, 1968, 1973, 1975). Finally, I shall cite new investigations that seriously challenge the old world view, and offer sounder guideposts for a reorientation in psychoanalytic literary criticism.

DIRECTIONS OF PSYCHOANALYTIC CRITICISM

Let me take note of the historical particulars. With relatively rare exceptions, such as Rank's (1932) radical departure from Freud on the nature of art and the artist, psychoanalysts have generally followed Freud's initial orientation as developed in two seminal papers, one on Jensen's Gradiva (1907) and the other entitled "Creative writers and day-dreaming" (1908). In these writings, Freud uses the daydream and dream as a paradigm for the literary work: forbidden wishes from unconscious, infantile fantasies of the oral, anal, phallic, and genital stages of development are given disguised expression. Whereas the dream affords this disguised expression through the dream work, or mechanisms of the primary process,[1] so that the forbidden wish is rarely recognizable in the manifest content, the work of art accomplishes the same end through using elements of aesthetic form to distract the audience. In both cases, the consciences or superegos of dreamer and audience are partially circumvented. The greatness of art then is the communication of powerful forces and fantasies within the artist's unconscious to the audience without their fully realizing it. Given this analogy of the dream to art, the psychoanalytic critic endeavors to ignore, or at best search through elements of form in a work to the "deeper," and of course to him more pertinent psychological content and meanings.

With this basic orientation serving as his polar star, the psychoanalyst has explored literature in three basic directions. As psychoanalysis has attained new complexities over the years, it has enabled the psycho-analytic critic to extend his forays in each of these directions. The more familiar undertaking has been to elucidate the universality in works of art of unconscious fantasies derived from the psychosexual stages of development. A classic example would be Ernest Jones's (1948) analysis of *Hamlet* in the light of the Oedipus complex. An early variation of this was the analyses of myths in literature as shared unconscious fantasies of particular sociocultural groups. Such mythic critics with this psycho-analytic orientation, the most prominent pioneers among whom were Otto Rank (1932) and Geza Roheim (1963), are to be distinguished from the vaster body of critics who use a mythic analysis as derived from anthropology, religion, ethnology, and linguistics. Still another dimen-sion to the psychoanalytic search for universal unconscious fantasy in art via the route of mythic exploration was added by Jung and his followers. The Jungian interest in archetypal figures and themes from the racial unconscious has been a major influence on literary criticism over the last half century, particularly in the work of such critics as Maud Bodkin (Hyman, 1948), Leslie Fiedler (1963), and Northrop Frye (1957).

A more recent preoccupation with universal unconscious fantasies in art, with important implications for criticism, is found in English schools of Freudian psychoanalysis, particularly in Melanie Klein and her followers. Here, unconscious fantasy is viewed as stemming from the interaction of a person's libidinal and aggressive drives with early familial interpersonal experiences or object relations. These early experiences are internalized in the psyche as internal objects (imagoes in traditional Freudian theory), and become the basis of unconscious fantasies supplementary to those derived from the psychosexual stages of development. While there has been considerable controversy over the particulars of Klein's contribution to psychoanalytic theory, her picture of the world of early object relations or psychosocial stages of development has struck a most responsive cord in modern psycho-analysis. Other major theorists such as Erik Erikson (1950), Ronald Fairbairn (1952), Edith Jacobson (1964), Heinz Kohut (1971), Margaret Mahler (1968), Rene Spitz (1965), Harry Stack Sullivan (1953), D. W. Winnicott (1965), among others have dramatically enlarged the knowledge of early object relations, so that this area is now an important part of contemporary Freudian as well as neo-Freudian psychoanalysis.

The implications of this broadening approach to early object relations and internalizations are several. For one, it makes available to the critic a far greater range of unconscious fantasy and emotional stages and experiences from childhood than the psychosexual only, which has figured so ubiquitously in psychoanalytic literary criticism. For another, it opens up a far broader study of the ego or self, with issues of self-image, identity, identification patterns, and narcissism, which has become the basis of the later work of the psychoanalytic critic, Norman Holland. As I shall allude to below, these concepts are far more relevant for the psychoanalytic critic in considering much of avant-garde drama for instance than the traditional psychosexual fantasies. In still another vein, explorations into the ego or self have profound implications for a new theory of the primary process, and thus creativity as well, with considerable ramifications for psychoanalytic literary criticism, which I shall discuss in the third section.

A brief example of a Kleinian contribution to applied psychoanalysis, that of Joan Riviere's commentary on Ibsen's *The Master-Builder*, is very much in order to illustrate its contrast with the more traditional use of psychosexual fantasies. In Riviere's (1957) analysis, a character such as Solness's wife is seen as both a character in herself and a representation of an internalized part of Solness's own psyche: the internalized mother who is destroyed by infantile greed. Hilda, too, is viewed as partly a manifestation of Solness: she is his "manic defense," denying all reality, particularly the destruction of his internalized object world. As important and novel as Riviere's analysis is, however, I must qualify that her contribution is still beset by the many-headed monster of psychological reductionism, i.e., there is no scanning of the rich imagery in the play for other levels of meaning with which the psychological viewpoint could be integrated, not to mention other aspects of form and structure.[2]

The second major direction in psychoanalytic literary criticism has been to investigate the unconscious motivation or psychopathology of a character in order to penetrate to the underlying meanings of a literary work. While earlier interpretations concentrated completely on character formation and motivation derived from the psychosexual stages of development, and most usually the Oedipal, later analyses have, with the newer contributions to psychoanalysis, become far more sophisticated. Thus, Phillip Weissman (1965) in a chapter of his book, *Creativity in the Theatre*, analyzes Tennessee Williams's prostitute heroines in terms of problems of early object relations as well as Oedipal difficulties. Kurt Eissler (1971) in his work, *On Hamlet and "Hamlet,"* also adds considerable refinement to our view of the dynamics of Hamlet's superego and ego ideal and the effect of these on dramatic action. Not only does Eissler try to use his understanding of Hamlet as a key to the exigencies of plot; he also sees the character as the embodiment of little understood universal laws of the psyche. This approach contrasts considerably with the older one of seeing a character in literature or drama as a completely real, living person, the bane of earlier critics from both psychoanalytic and literary backgrounds.

The third and final direction that psychoanalytic criticism took, starting with Freud's work on Leonardo da Vinci, has been to relate the hidden psychological meanings in the work of art (either the unconscious fantasies or the analysis of character) to the author's life. An example of this is Kligerman's (1962) work relating *Six Characters in Search of an Author* to Pirandello's life and personality. At its worst, treating the work of art as a chapter in the creator's psychobiography led to the reductionistic position that art, itself, is a manifestation of psychopathology, and can be understood simply by understanding the vicissitudes of an author's childhood. At its best, a sophisticated psychobiographical approach can help shed additional light on an author's work, and has been used to good effect by such a distinguished critic as Leon Edel (1953) on Henry James.

Thus briefly reviewing the directions in which the psychoanalytic critic has set sail, it is time to assess some of the efforts of his forays. There is little doubt that a more sophisticated and penetrating psychoanalytic understanding of unconscious fantasy, of issues of the self and identity, of the wellsprings of character, and of the author's biography can all be of considerable value to criticism. But as Crews (1976) rightly noted, an increase of psychoanalytic knowledge and a sharpening of the analyst's tools may only help dig deeper the ditch of reductionism. The issue still remains as to the uses of psychoanalysis in the critical endeavor. Even with significant advances in psychoanalytic knowledge, all too often the psychoanalyst has still equated the work of art with the dream and daydream, and continued his search for latent psychological meaning as the be-all and end-all of his efforts. In this, he has often been supported by major psychoanalytic views on form and creativity that more often than not have subtly carried over Freud's basic assumptions.

AESTHETIC FORM AND CREATIVITY

I would now like to turn to important psychoanalytic contributions to the theories of aesthetic form and creativity to assess the degree to which these approaches reinforce or contradict Freud's basic assumptions on aesthetics, and thus to the basic orientation of psychoanalytic literary criticism (Bush, 1967). Early psychoanalysts, such as Sachs (1942), basically followed Freud's view of form as disguise, but developed it in a more sophisticated way. While Sachs viewed form in art as more elaborate than in the dream, he also saw it as a gateway to unconscious content, art thus restoring to the ego dissociated parts of the personality. His approach naturally led in the same direction as Freud's in searching for unconscious content. Of the early analysts, and perhaps the later ones too, Rank (1932) departed most radically from Freud's basic assumptions on form. He saw form in a dual way: as the search for ego mastery over death in the artist's quest for immortality, and as the synthesis of the dualism between the individual and his society, form bearing the stamp of the collectivity. This latter concept of form presaged the important work of later analysts such as Kris (1952) and Alexander (1963).

Kris, coming to psychoanalysis from the field of art history, enlarged Freud's earlier conception of form as disguise and distraction by seeing it as partly determined by the conventions of culture and as a means of socially adaptive expression by the artist. Alexander also predicated changes in artistic style and form upon the fluctuating social climate; e.g., the movement into nonobjective art and literature as closely tied to a general disillusionment in the Western world in the twentieth century, resulting in a regressive turning within. Implicit in the work of

Rank, Kris, and Alexander is the artist's conscious or unconscious identifications with certain groups of the collectivity in a particular historical period, which is then manifested in his work through its form and style.[3] Rycroft (1975) extends this notion to the artist's identification with and use of the symbols of the collectivity and other artists, rather than his own purely private ones, as in dreams.

The main impetus in more modern psychoanalytic approaches to aesthetic form, comes, however, from the contributions of psycho-analytic ego psychology, particularly Ernst Kris's (1952) theory of creativity. Kris's views on art and creativity are generally looked upon as the most definitive ones in psychoanalytic circles, and have had considerable influence on art critics such as Gombrich (1957) and Ehrenzweig (1967), and literary critics such as Hoffman (1957), Lesser (1957), and Holland (1964, 1968, 1973, 1975). Kris reinforced the bond between art work and dream work by equating artistic ambiguity, an important concept of the "new critic," William Empson (1930), with the overdetermination[4] of the primary process. Thus, the many-leveled meanings of a work of art are considered as basically similar to the overdetermined meanings of the primary process, as manifested in symptoms or a dream. In like manner, Kris also equated poetic metaphor, an integration of different levels of experience, with the metaphorical expression of dream imagery, where one presentation analogously stands for some more unconscious meaning of the latent content. He envisages the artist as regressing "in the service of his ego" to the imagery of the primary process with its variety of meanings, and then as progressing to the rational ego where secondary-process thinking cast derivatives from this primary-process exploration into aesthetic form. Rose (1980), on the other hand, sees aesthetic form as serving to transform contradictions into a dynamic unity while preserving the unique integrity of contrasting elements – such as primary and secondary process, constancy and change, emotional impulses and intellectual thought, and self and social reality. He does not attend to form as giving meanings.

Marshall Bush (1967), in an essay, "The problem of form in the psychoanalytic theory of art," summarizes the perspectives of Kris (1952) and other ego psychologists such as Heinz Hartmann (1964), Ives Hendrick (1942), David Rappaport (1951), and Robert White (1964). Bush derives from these contributions the conclusions that aesthetic form is a very high order of achievement of various ego functions and can be appreciated in its own right; and form is involved in an organic integration of diverse elements of content, analogous to the ego's attempt to integrate aspects of the id, superego, and outer reality into a workable synthesis. The implications for literary criticism, according to Bush, are on the one hand psychological support for an appreciation of the formalist approach to aesthetics; and on the other, supplementary to the traditional psychoanalytic search for underlying psychological meanings and content, a further appreciation of the transformation, organization, and resolution of unconscious content through the manifestations of high-order ego functioning in aesthetic form.

The psychoanalytic view of form clearly pulls in two directions. To the extent that aesthetic form is related to the conventions, symbols, and historical changes in the collectivity, psychoanalytic understanding can enlarge upon the more universal meanings that are the essence of literary endeavor. However, when form is viewed as primarily the ego's conflict involved way of handling and transforming unconscious material, in however elegant or refined a manner, the psychoanalyst tends once again to sift through the ego mechanisms (form) to the more unconscious or underlying psychological meanings as his final goal. And when this is reinforced by such a universally accepted theory of creativity as Kris's, that centrally locates creativity in the primary process, thus binding art work and dream work more closely together, then reductionism in psychoanalytic criticism becomes even more rampant. The possibility that the artist's ego could function in a relatively conflict-free way to produce new meanings seems to be almost completely ignored by these psychoanalytic critics.

The Kleinians (Segal, 1957), as is their wont, have a significantly different approach to creativity and thus to the function of form, one that is in some ways closer to certain literary theories. They view the central motivation for creativity as stemming from the child's need to make reparation to the maternal object during the depressive stage.[5] If the creative act is thus to encompass destructive impulses, form is broadly considered as introducing order into chaos; in tragedy, order is based on the paradigm of the reparation and restitution experience of early infancy resolving destructive impulses toward the mother. The Kleinians' use of this paradigm of early childhood seems oriented toward the broader view of Kenneth Burke (1941) in his chapter, "Beauty and the Sublime," that literature encompasses threat, the poet being likened to a medicine man who deals with poisons, but gives them in salutary doses. Undoubtedly, some of the more current-day ego-psychological views described just above can also lend psychological credence to Burke's perspective on literary transformation.

Other approaches to creativity encompass a strong emphasis on symbolization and the preconscious (Deri, 1984; Feirstein, 1997; and Kubie, 1958, 1978). Then, there is the interesting work of Chasseguet-Smirgal (1984) who sees creativity in artists as frequently related to perversion in the broad sense of a disavowal of the father's penis, with a fixation on an anal penis and an idealization of aesthetics.

CRITICS' USE OF PSYCHOANALYSIS

How has the literary critic used psychoanalysis, and to what extent have these major mappings of psychoanalysis influenced him? From the second decade of the twentieth century psychoanalysis has indeed had considerable influence on important literary critics such as Kenneth Burke (1953), Lionel Trilling (1963), Stanley Edgar Hyman (1948), William Empson (1930), Robert Gorham Davis (1963), and Maud Bodkin (Hyman, 1948). For this generation of critics, psychoanalysis has been useful in a few main ways. One is to call attention to primary-process mechanisms of displacement (splitting of characters, reversals, double entendres, and such), condensation, and symbolism, and as these mechanisms are involved in poetic diction, atmosphere, and setting. Burke in particular sees the structure of a literary work determined in part by unconscious factors. He analyzes these by careful scrutiny of the clustering and equations of images taken within the context of a given work, or throughout the works of a writer.[6] Thus, important incongruities may arise between an author's overt intention and imagery that unwittingly conveys other meanings. I should note parenthetically that this close textual analysis of images, as well as of various other linguistic structures, is the hallmark of the French psychoanalytic approach to criticism. But, however much Burke stresses unconscious factors, he became rather critical of psychoanalytic literary criticism in its almost ubiquitous neglect of factors of form and communication, and of a variety of other meanings than the psychological, a criticism to which this chapter is fully sympathetic.

Still other uses of psychoanalysis have been to delve into a character's motivation, or of defended against psychosexual fantasies, such as in Empson's analysis of the symbolism in *Alice's Adventures in Wonderland*; or of the important use of archetypal themes by Maud Bodkin. Then there is the important issue of the psychology of form as communication. In a critic strongly oriented toward psychoanalysis, such as Simon O. Lesser (1957), form is viewed as giving pleasure and/or regulating anxiety. This is in contrast to Burke's broader appraisal of the psychological function of form as the arousal and satisfaction of the audience's appetites, but in a refined and eloquent transcendence of emotions.

Three literary critics have pushed the boundaries of psychoanalytic literary criticism further in comprehensive attempts to integrate literary criticism with psychoanalysis, and in evolving theories of criticism strongly derived from psychoanalysis. Frederick Hoffman (1957) does this in "Psychology and literature," an appendix to his important book, *Freudianism and the Literary Mind*; Simon O. Lesser (1957) in *Fiction and the Unconscious*; and Norman Holland in his *Psychoanalysis and Shakespeare* (1964), and more thoroughly in his *Dynamics of Literary Response* (1968), *Poems in Persons: An Introduction to the Psychoanalysis of Literature* (1973), and *5 Readers Reading* (1975). All three are considerably knowledgeable in traditional Freudian psychoanalysis, and all have been strongly influenced by the work of Ernst Kris. Since Holland's work is the most comprehensive of the three, and the most influential on the American critical scene, I shall evaluate his attempt to elaborate a new aesthetic based on psychoanalysis as developed in his *Dynamics of Literary Response*.

For Holland, artistic form is a valid, but nonetheless defensive transformation of unconscious impulses and fantasies from the various psychosexual stages of development into intellectual, moral, social, and religious meanings. His model comes from Kris's theory of creativity, of primary process being integrated with aesthetic considerations, socially or culturally determined. It is also based on the psychoanalytic structural model of the mind, particularly of compromises between the ego defenses and the id fantasies wrought by the anxiety-provoking power of the cultural restrictions internalized in the superego. Considerations of early object relations and various aspects of the self were originally conspicuous by their absence, but in his later work, *5 Readers Reading* – influenced by Lichtenstein's (1977) work on identity – they are much more fully present. In any case, Holland's theory is basically a conflict-oriented one and tends to view the literary work as a special type of compromise formation, not totally unlike the formation of a symptom.

The explicitness with which Holland tries to relate aesthetic dimensions to his basic model of psychoanalysis, something the psychoanalytic critic has usually neglected to do, is the most salient feature of his contribution. Thus, he views form as a structure tending to inhibit underlying fantasies, in contrast to the dimension of language, which distracts the superego to enable the underlying fantasies to gain expression. Meaning, on the other hand, is seen more as facilitating sublimation of fantasies than as an inhibitor of them. The reader's or spectator's identification with a fictional character is in order to serve either a defense or a wish, depending on the particular traits of the character. Affects that are aroused by a work of literature cluster around four categories of drive satisfactions, derived from the four stages of psychosexual development: oral, anal, phallic, and genital, combined with the presence or absence in the reader of anxiety and arousal, and on whether his defenses are strong or weak. This is a much more detailed working out of Lesser's concept of form as primarily giving pleasure and/or regulating anxiety.

Holland's basic approach, then, is to penetrate through form, meanings, and imagery to the underlying psychosexual fantasies that "fuel" the literary work, and then to appreciate how the formal aesthetic elements either allow them expression or inhibit them, inciting the reader to experience his own fantasies and defenses. Thus, Holland emphasizes the communicative nature of art, and the psychological nature of the aesthetic experience, usually neglected by the psychoanalytic critic, and about which Freud (1915) wrote only one paper, published posthumously in 1942. However important Holland's contributions are in his emphasis on the aesthetic experience and communication, his starting-point nevertheless is still the Freudian notion of the dream and daydream dressed in aesthetics. The more sophisticated note that Holland strikes, that aesthetic form is defensive transformation rather than disguise, simply results in a newer, much more subtle, and more thorough reductionism. Then there is Crews' (1976) incisive critique that Holland and other similar psychoanalytic critics have lost sight of art as being primarily meaning-creating.

A NEW INTEGRATION

As persistent and pervasive as is the correlation of the literary work with the daydream and dream in applied psychoanalysis and psychoanalytic literary criticism, it can nevertheless be seriously challenged by Albert Rothenberg's (1979) work on the processes of creativity in highly recognized writers, and by my own work on dreams, art, and creativity as elaborated in Chapters 4 and 5. The central issue is that the literary work has much higher levels of integration than dream imagery, and aims at more universal meanings rather than particularized biographical ones. The literary work thus attains and expresses artistic meanings noticeably absent in the dream. More specifically, as I have carefully demonstrated, poetic metaphor, so crucial to the broader meanings in a literary work, is present in the dream in only incipient forms. It thus becomes apparent that Kris (1952) wandered astray in equating poetic metaphor and metaphorical expression in dreams, the latter standing analogously for unconscious meanings in the latent content, with the former expressing a high-level integration of the concrete and abstract. Similarly, upon careful scrutiny, it is possible to discern the elements for the making of paradoxes in the latent content of a dream, but never the real integration expressing the paradox.[7] Whatever true integration of antithetical elements from the latent content does take place is from the conscious creative work of analyst and analyzand within the context of current psychical problems in the patient's life and/or therapy, as I have delineated in Chapter 3. In considering literature and the dream, Coleridge's "extremes meet" is pertinent. But if literature is to be differentiated from the dream, then this declaration must be amended to "extremes meet meaningfully."

Rothenberg's work makes unmistakably clear that the integration of diverse meanings in a literary work through its various symbols and metaphors is of a qualitatively different nature from condensation in dream imagery, where there is little if any true integration of the component parts, and where meanings are derived from the dreamer's associations rather than from those of the listener. Thus, Kris's facile equation of ambiguity in literature with the overdetermination of the primary process is but a chimera that has tended to lure critic as well as analyst astray. Rothenberg, in ongoing studies of highly creative writers, has been able to identify a thought process that he terms "'Janusian thinking', crucial to literary creativity, in enabling the writer to make high-level integrations of two or more antithetical elements." An example he (1969) cites is O'Neill's use of multiple antithetical elements around the themes of salvation, death, and sexuality in *The Iceman Cometh*. Since this cognitive ability clearly transcends primary-process thinking, he relates it to an imaginative or refined part of the secondary process, or what he sometimes terms as translogical cognitive processes. This must be emphasized as a radical change from Kris and other psychoanalytic theorists like Noy (1969) who place so much of the creative process in primary-process thinking.

Rothenberg's findings clearly imply a rerouting of the basic assumptions underlying psychoanalytic literary criticism. They lend a psychological underpinning to the validity of the multiple meanings in a literary work in their fullest complexity, that should obviate the usual psychological gymnastics of trying to find the hidden primary-process conflicts or varied sublimating mechanisms. Thus, the abstract meanings of a literary work can be accorded a psychological legitimacy rarely acknowledged by the psychoanalytic critic.

Have I now reached the point of asserting that applied psychoanalysis and psychoanalytic literary criticism have gone so completely astray that there is little hope of any significant psychoanalytic contribution to literary explorations? Hardly so. There are obviously a variety of ways that psychoanalytic understanding has been and can be judiciously used in criticism. What perhaps needs further clarifying is, on the one hand, the use of form and structure by the psychoanalytic critic; and, on the other, the integration of insights derived from in-depth analysis of character and relationship with other meanings of a work. I see no real need to amend a more literary view, such as Burke's (1941a) that form in its broadest sense communicates the richness of intellectual synthesis and emotional integration in their fullest complexity, rather than as merely facilitating the expression or inhibition of infantile fantasies. In fact, Rothenberg (1973) in a study of O'Neill's *Long Day's Journey into Night* and Miller's *A View from the Bridge* revises Holland's "form is defense" to "defense is part of form:" the playwright's handling of the defenses of his characters becomes an important regulator of dramatic tension.

The psychoanalytic critic can often use a variety of formal and structural elements in a work, when merited, for psychological meanings. These meanings, of course, do not in any way degrade other viewpoints derived from the formal elements, but are rather supplementary; and in fact, should be integrated with them, a task more often than not ignored by the psychoanalytic critic. Chapter 7 on Pirandello's *Six Characters in Search of an Author* and *Henry IV* by Roland and Rizzo is one example of this approach.

In *Six Characters* we took into account innovative, anti-naturalistic elements such as the impotent and repudiating position of the playwright; the lack of any three-dimensional characterization; the unique and incongruous juxtaposition of two-dimensional, imaginary characters existing in fantasy-like time and space with a supposedly real, but one-dimensional stage company; and a dramatic technique of alienation – the actors constantly stepping out of their roles. We also assessed the central metaphor of the quest of the imaginary characters for an existence, and the major paradox that although the six characters are more real than the stage company, they depend on the latter for their embodiment and realization. (For a detailed discussion of some of the meanings of these formal and structural elements, see Chapter 7 in this book.)

The absence of three-dimensional characters in *Six Characters in Search of an Author* is thus perfectly consonant with the vision of an unrealized self. In a similar vein, Martin Esslin (1961) noted that part of Beckett's significant contribution was to find a new dramatic form and structure to incorporate the existential visions of Sartre and Camus around the vanishing self, which they themselves could not render dramatically effective because of their dependence on more traditional, naturalistic portrayals.

Still another example of an innovative change in form involving characterization that cries for psychological elucidation is Pinter's *The Homecoming*. As I describe in detail in Chapter 8, the key to following the play's seemingly absurd dramatic action is recognition of the character, Ruth, as both a character and non-character simultaneously. She is both a real character, in herself, and acts as a puppet pulled by the strings of the unconscious, living imagoes in the five men of the dead wife and mother, Jesse. Thus, the psychoanalytic concept of identification as the internalization within the psyche of early patterned interactions within the family is invaluable for understanding important aspects of the dramatic action in *The Homecoming*, which otherwise has baffled critic and audience alike.

Lest it be imagined that the approach envisioned here is only applicable to more avant-garde drama where the important meanings of the formal elements are often broadly psychological in nature, I would like to illustrate how Riviere's (1957) psychoanalytic analysis of Ibsen's *The Master-Builder*, if integrated with other meaning of the work, helps amplify it. In any truly adequate criticism of *The Master-Builder*, dimensions must be elucidated of the place of the drama in Ibsen's work, and its relationship to his life; its relationship to Ibsen's sociohistorical values, such as the emphasis on self-realization and humanism versus outworn religious and other traditional doctrines; literary and mythic themes of the older man's search for youth and revitalization, and the sacrificial figure of Solness at the end with a wreath over his head; the plight of the creative artist in society; and the various aesthetic and dramatic devices used. However, I shall focus mainly on the central paradox of the builder of homes being a destroyer of homes.

On one hand, we have presented to us a great builder of churches and then homes – specially designed for their occupants. Whatever luck came Solness's way, he was undoubtedly a man of considerable talent, an artist. Moreover, the desolation of his own family can be easily taken on one level as the personal sacrifices of the creative artist, and his challenge to God as a movement toward more modern values of humanism and self-realization. Why then is there such a need for youth and rejuvenation, and such feelings of persecution when he is at the top and so greatly sought after? Here the psychological analysis of Riviere is very pertinent: he is a man possessed by the ambition of infantile greed, which has caused inner desolation and persecutory anxieties. His downfall is brought about not by his building or creating, but rather by his power urges to climb to the top. His images of his building are not involved in his destruction, only those of his climbing to the top.[8] Thus, art and power become too intertwined. Throughout the play, it is reported how he has struggled to the very top from a poor background. And it is finally Hilda, who comes to him in hiking clothes with fantasies of his ascending ever higher, and who urges him to climb the tower in spite of his terror of heights, which brings about his destruction. Thus, the creative builder becomes the destroyer when too infused by power drives, which stem from infantile greed. This may then be viewed as a metaphor for industrial man, who abdicates his human needs for the lure of power drives.

In a very limited way, I have tried to show how the psychoanalytic critic can use important aspects of form for psychological meanings, when psychological meanings seem appropriate, and to integrate these meanings into a fuller analysis of a work. In like manner, the psychoanalytic critic may help clarify emotional communication as well. An example of this is Pirandello's use of alienation, wherein an actor involves the audience in his role, and then suddenly steps out of it. This original dramatic device induces in the audience the very feeling of being split that is also being communicated abstractly. Humor in Pirandello also serves in a related vein in emotionally involving the audience while simultaneously subtly drawing their attention to the incongruities and splits that are taking place. I may add, parenthetically, that the whole issue of humor in the Theater of the Absurd and its evocative communicative effects on the audience needs further study and elucidation.

However, the communication of emotion and fantasy in literature is a more profound issue for the psychoanalytic critic than the above discussion alludes to, and merits careful exploration. Holland's (1968) proposition that fantasies underlie literary works and emotionally fuel them is a most valuable one. But it needs radical amending both as to the nature of fantasies or emotional states that are involved, and to a methodology to integrate them with the other meanings of a work.

As I have delineated in Chapter 4, an expanded understanding of the primary process not only includes the traditional notion of allowing forbidden wishes of psychosexual fantasies to evade the superego for disguised expression, but also that the primary process gives excellent metaphorical expression to widely different facets of the psyche, such as varied aspects of the ego and self, superego and ego-ideal, internal objects and other internalizations, and developmental stages and states of mind. The traditional use of the primary process if employed analytically for a limited dimension in a work, such as in Doubrovsky's (1978) analysis of the card game in Sartre's *La Nausée*, renders clearer some of the affectual nature of a work. But as a be-all and end-all in itself, it results in what Crews (1976) terms the debunking propensity.

From this expanded version of the primary process, it is easy to see that fantasies fueling a literary work can be expanded far beyond those dealing with psychosexuality alone. But elucidating these fantasies or emotional states is not the end-point of the psychoanalytic critic's search and research. Rather, it is to integrate them with the broader and more universal meanings of the work, and to show how they are interrelated.

But to be able to use this valuable asset judiciously requires theorizing on the nature of the creative process, particularly the integration of primary- and secondary-process thinking. As I have described in Chapter 5, artists' expression of their inner world through primary-process imagery is yoked to their artistic visions, poetic metaphors, and paradoxes of their work; that is, to its more universal, social meanings.

My perspective differs from Holland in that I see emotional states in literature as enabling the audience to experience emotionally on an individual level the artistic vision being communicated on a more abstract level, through various structures and formal elements. Thus, the task of the psychoanalytic critic is to use his or her in-depth understanding of these underlying emotional states in their organic relationship to the artistic purposes and vision of a work, rather than as end-points in themselves.[9] Or it may even be the lot of the psychoanalytic critic to point out that the underlying emotional fantasies may contradict the more abstract meanings, if such be the case.

In summary, psychoanalytic literary criticism has most often been shipwrecked by the dual dangers of psychological reductionism and of ignorance of psychoanalysis or aesthetics. The latter danger is one of the built-in risks of any interdisciplinary effort, and can be overcome only by increased knowledge of the other's field and/or close collaboration. The former danger essentially derives from following the very prevalent but fallacious assumption relating the literary work to the daydream and dream. I have tried to cite newer formulations around the dream and art, and on the creative process, that help highlight the significant distinctions between the literary work and the dream. It is my hope that the new perspective will enable the psychoanalytic critic to use his psychoanalytic knowledge to enhance rather than reduce the integrity and vision of a work of art.

NOTES

1. Primary-process thinking involves mechanisms of displacement – such as affect manifesting itself in areas other than where it belongs, reversal, and the like; condensation of incorporating into one image a variety of diverse, unintegrated meanings, derived from the dreamer's associations; and symbolism – conveying basic aspects of the id.
2. Riviere, besides ignoring other major dimensions of the play such as the plight of the artist in society, self-realization and humanism versus outworn religious and

traditional doctrines, mythical themes of the older man's search for youth and revitalization, and the sacrificial figure of Solness, also neglected the main paradox of the play – the builder of homes being a destroyer of homes, as well as the varied imagery around climbing. Riviere's contribution would have undoubtedly been much more significant for serious criticism if she had attempted to integrate her work with any of these other dimensions of the play.

3. Kenneth Burke (1941a) introduces the same formulation by citing Pope's highly refined verse as related to the etiquette of a newly propertied class to which he belonged.

4. Overdetermination refers to the economic way in which the unconscious attaches a variety of meanings and motives to a particular image or symptom. The symptom is regarded as an unconscious compromise-formation of conflicting motives, whereas images in dreams are often a condensation of a variety of often unrelated thoughts and meanings, adduced by the dreamer's associations to the image. Such unconscious, non-logical, imagistic thinking is known as the primary process.

5. In Kleinian theory, once the infant has internalized sufficient experiences of the good mother to be able to see her as a whole, and his aggression as stemming from himself, he experiences guilt over his aggression and then needs to make reparations to the mother.

6. This methodology contrasts with the psychoanalytic analysis of dreams whereby the patient associates to the images in the dream, and these associations are then given meaning within the context of the patient's life and/or therapy relationship.

7. Since almost everything upon this earth has an exception to the rule, the dream is no exception. There are indeed the very rare, creative dreams that do express a poetic metaphor or paradox, or an unusual scientific discovery. But these are explained by even Freud as being carried over lock, stock, and barrel from the preconscious creative processes of daytime, rather than as being intrinsic to dream work.

8. I am indebted to Professor Gary Keller for pointing out this distinction in an interdisciplinary drama seminar at the National Psychological Association for Psychoanalysis.

9. Burke (1953, p. 83) has a somewhat similar formulation in discussing Coleridge's poem, "Dejection." "The poet would convey a sense of political foreboding. To do so effectively, he draws upon his own deepest experiences of foreboding."

7

Psychoanalysis in Search of Pirandello: *Six Characters* and *Henry IV*

SIX CHARACTERS

Few dramatic works have so challenged the modern imagination as Pirandello's *Six Characters in Search of an Author* and *Henry IV*. Over the years, critics and audiences have endeavored to understand these enigmatic and profoundly psychological works only to discover still deeper and more complex layers of meaning. It is hardly surprising, then, that the better known of the two works, *Six Characters*, has attracted a flurry of critical attention based on psychoanalysis (Bentley, 1968; Jacobs, 1974; Kligerman, 1962; Wangh, 1976), a dimension of psychology not so readily available to an earlier generation of Pirandello critics.

To assess the contributions of the psychoanalytic critic is to confront the promise and the problems of traditional applied psychoanalysis; even more pertinent is the need for a more valid critical endeavor that can still encompass psychoanalysis. The most fruitful of the insights generated by a psychoanalytic approach has been Kligerman's (1962) study of the inner plot of the six characters, a strategy generated by Ernest Jones's (1948) analysis of the play-within-the-play in *Hamlet*. This analysis in turn reflects the importance ascribed by Freud (1900) to the dream-within-the-dream, a structure which classical psychoanalysis interprets as yielding the fullest and deepest expression of infantile fantasies, wishes, and conflicts. Kligerman insightfully assessed the inner plot and the six characters as expressing qualities of the primary process, in contrast to the full development of character and the rationality of dramatic action characteristic of the secondary process. He was then able to delineate a variety of infantile psychological themes.

The promise of this psychoanalytic approach became transformed into a problem in criticism the moment Kligerman (1962, p. 732) dismissed the rest of the play as being of little consequence – mere "comic badinage between actors and characters, and a great deal of philosophical discussion of reality and art . . ." Wangh (1976) and Jacobs (1974)[1] followed suit, but differed in their interpretations of the inner plot; the former stressed pathological Oedipal jealousy, while the latter focused on pre-Oedipal deprivation. The extreme emphasis laid by these critics upon the inner plot can now be dismissed as mere exaggeration reflecting their concern with plumbing the depths of the psyche rather than subjecting the artistic work to critical analysis. This emphasis stems from an explicit psychoanalytic assumption that the greatness of a literary work lies not in its artistic vision and the aesthetic experience it affords, but rather in the author's ability to communicate on a subliminal level to his audience intense and universal unconscious infantile conflicts.

Another major cul-de-sac into which the Pirandellian psychoanalyst-critic has unwittingly wandered is the formulation that form and structure basically function as defensive transformations of infantile fantasies.[2] Thus Wangh viewed the particular amalgamation of structures in *Six Characters* as a layering of resistances to disguise and defend against the expression of intense infantile conflicts and passions. This type of analysis adds little to our overall understanding of the play as an artistic and dramatic work; at best, it serves to illumine the inner struggles of the playwright.

As the psychoanalyst-critic is beleaguered by problems in aesthetics, the drama critic interested in psychoanalysis is beset by the complexity of new contributions in the field. Eric Bentley first initiated a more valid critical approach by incorporating the insights of Kligerman with attempts to encompass the philosophical discussions and the total dramatic action of *Six Characters*. But in turning to the "avant-garde" position of R. D. Laing (1965), Bentley (1968, p. 71) analyzes *Six Characters* as being concerned with schizophrenia. "I am arguing that it is not a philosophical play at all because the philosophy is harnessed to a non-philosophical chariot. *The content is psychopathological from beginning to end*" (my italics). Bentley concludes by drawing attention to the dialectical relationship existing between the indeterminate nature of the six characters with their loose temporal and spatial contexts, and the utter one-dimensional concreteness of actors and director moving within a clear specificity of time and place. But he is content to observe that as indeterminate as the six characters are, they are ironically far less one-dimensional than the supposed "real" personages drawn from life; and that this reversal functions as one of the play's major comic devices.

Are we then justified in averring that *Six Characters in Search of an Author* is a play about schizophrenia? Or even that it is about pathological jealousy or emotional deprivation? We think not. In our judgment, *Six Characters* explores modern man's fate in a way far more extensive and profound than a work primarily engaged in studying individual forms of psychopathology. A more valid use of psychoanalysis in Pirandello criticism would maintain the critic's sensitivity to the subtleties of form and structure, while incorporating the contemporary psychoanalyst's knowledge in the areas of identity and the self. A thoughtful examination of the structure of *Six Characters* is very much to the point in beginning our analysis, to be followed by important, recent considerations on the nature of splitting.

Six Characters unfolds within the shell of naturalistic form. Six characters appear at the premises of an acting company who are rehearsing the Pirandello play, *Rules of the Game.* The characters become involved in a dramatic encounter depicting their desperate attempts to become realized on stage after their author has repudiated them. Naturalistic structure and dramatic tension are initially sustained by the characters' efforts to persuade the company's manager to stage them. Their endeavor meets with success, and they then proceed to enact the drama of their own story. But naturalism, as it is generally understood, ceases at this point to provide the dominant dramatic structure.

The play's anti-naturalist stance is exemplified by the position of the author in relation to the play. The Pirandellian author fails to assume his classical role as teacher, prophet, or as central intelligence; rather the playwright is now disclosed as being impotent and repudiating. Rejection of the naturalistic mode is further evidenced by the fact that the six characters are in themselves only two-dimensional figures unlike the characters found in naturalistic drama; indeed, the actors, manager, and stagehands are one step further removed from the dominant mode in that they are but one-dimensional stereotypes. The play is thus totally unsuited to method techniques of any kind and hardly lends itself to complex forms of characterization.

The movement in dramatic form from naturalistic to anti-naturalistic structure is significant in that it allows the characters to project themselves as psychological processes, rather than as characterization suitable for individual, depth-psychological analysis. As Bentley noted, the six characters exist within a paradoxical situation. While they are far more real and passionate than the members of the acting company, they nevertheless exist within a fantasy, primary-process realm in contrast to the "real" secondary-process universe of the acting company. In this fashion, the play's two levels of reality are linked to each other within a structure of juxtaposition and overriding incongruity. Moreover, there is the further paradox that while the six characters are more real than the stage company, they nevertheless utterly depend on the latter for their realization.

As the naturalistic action progresses, we gradually find ourselves standing in a hallway of mirrors where multilevel vantage points reflect reality's many facets. Thus, a considerable part of the incongruous interaction between actors, manager, and characters could have occurred just as easily in Act II as in Act III, and vice versa. As Kligerman astutely observed, only the inner plot involving the six characters demonstrates a highly structured development.

Other modifications of naturalistic structure may be found in any number of experimental devices introduced by Pirandello into the dramatic structure. First, we note that all the actors in the cast and particularly the six characters experience a marked sense of alienation from their roles. From roles played to thoroughly engrossed audiences, the actors suddenly step forth as persons, thereby destroying the traditional illusion of character. Second, we observe that the play is presented as process – it is presented in the making, unfolding contemporaneously with the desperate search of the six characters for existence and embodiment. Then, the work has been termed a comedy although its incongruities are not only humorous but painful and tragic as well. In this way, the old form of comedy is transformed into what may properly be called a "grotesque."[3]

Overt themes in *Six Characters* deal with the nature of theater and the creative process. More specifically, the play expresses the conflicts between the author and his work, and between the work and its meaningful embodiment on stage. However, we see this exploration into the life of the theater not as an end in itself, but rather as paradoxically related to life itself, which is theater. Pirandello's choice of only one- and two-dimensional characters at once suggests an exploration of the psychological processes and existential dilemmas which beset twentieth-century man.

The psychoanalyst might well object that such an approach ignores profound psychological considerations. *The aim of our methodology, however, will be to use psychoanalysis to elucidate the psychological aspects of the play's central metaphors, paradoxes, and structures – those symbolic forms that make the work universal – rather than to isolate psychological content as an end unto itself.*[4] Thus we seek to integrate the "depth" approach of psychoanalysis with more properly literary ends to achieve what we consider a valid form of psychoanalytic literary criticism.

With this orientation in mind, it becomes evident that the inner drama of the six characters in quest of author and existence must be viewed not only in terms of its psychological import, but as a crucial metaphor as well as structural element of intrinsic value in and of itself. As projections of the creative imagination and symbolic expressions of the inner self juxtaposed with social role, the six characters assume an importance that transcends the limits of their own drama. By contrast, Shakespeare's "play-within-the-play" in *Hamlet*, integral as it is to the work, is of far less consequence as an overall structural element than the inner plot of *Six Characters*.

Prior to interpreting *Six Characters*, we must clarify "splitting," a key psychoanalytic concept of considerable complexity. Splitting involves many of the most salient contributions of contemporary psychoanalysis, ones highly relevant to an understanding of Pirandello, with distinctions to be made that have yet to be discussed in psychoanalytic literary criticism.

One well-known definition of the term refers to the splitting of a single character into two or more others. The operation involves the primary-process mechanism of displacement and may be utilized to sharpen characterization. The notion of splitting has been understood and applied over the years by a number of psychoanalytically oriented critics, first and foremost Kenneth Burke (1941b) in "Freud and the analysis of poetry." A refinement in our understanding of splitting by displacement is to be found in a paper published by Sheppard and Saul (1958). Their findings have suggested to us that the splitting of characters by displacement occurs at times not merely for fuller dramatic effect, but as encompassing important defensive mechanisms. Thus, where a particular character may display the socially approved facets of a given personality structure, any number of other characters may express its reprehensible and blameworthy aspects. Splitting by displacement then is an indispensable methodological tool to understand both the significance of the inner drama of the six characters and the play as a whole.

A more recent interpretation of splitting – one that differs radically from the primary-process mechanism of displacement – is associated with concepts of identity and the self. In the popular as well as literary imagination, splitting is frequently equated with schizophrenia. But while the notion of schizophrenia as a metaphor for the madness of modern life may be highly evocative, it may also distract from clarifying the real nature of social madness.

Splitting as related to identity and the self is indeed a complex issue, but we may delineate directions most relevant to *Six Characters* and *Henry IV* by drawing upon the significant work of a variety of analysts who have explored this area, such as Erikson (1968), the Menakers (1965), R. D. Laing (1965), H. Lichtenstein (1977), Helen Lynd (1958), Schachtel (1961), Searles (1966), and Winnicott (1965); and later, Kernberg (1975) and Kohut (1977, 1984).

Splitting has a variety of faces, but they all eventually involve crucial defects in that essential psychological achievement, a meaningful and fulfilling adult identity: that is, the integration of vital aspects of the inner self with the multiple options of social role, at least in Western cultures. Thus, the individual strives to integrate the inner self of childhood and adolescence with commitment and involvement with major adult social roles (in love, friendship, and work), value systems, and the dominant skills of a given era (Erikson, 1968). Such identity syntheses by no means imply adjustment only to a given society, but often striving to change prevailing patterns of life. Except for the rare individual who can stand alone, however, identity is sustained and developed through repeated reciprocal relationships, where supportive reactions of others mirror back to the person whom he or she is trying to be. Thus, identity, while being profoundly individual, paradoxically matures only within the society of others.

Serious splits in the self may develop from two broad directions; each can seriously impair a fulfilling identity. One involves historical eras such as the present, of rapid, pervasive changes throughout society. For the psychoanalyst and critic to comment on such changes in depth without the collaboration of the historian and social scientist would obviously be presumptuous. However, certain broad outlines seem already clear. When major patterns of social life change extremely rapidly, and certain supportive systems disintegrate while others become highly impersonal; and when value systems, too, become fragmented, outmoded, or denigrated, then involvement with and commitment to social role and value system become much more difficult. Further, little supportive mirroring from others may cause great strife in the individual in his effort to maintain a meaningful identity synthesis. Thus, painful splitting may be then experienced between social role and the inner self.

Even when new societal interrelations become more flexible, and new opportunities are forthcoming, splitting may result. In these cases, the new roles may be at considerable variance with expectations and values internalized during childhood from the social reality of another generation. A case in point are the rapidly changing opportunities for women to combine serious career commitments with marriage and motherhood – a new dual-role identity often at considerable odds with the older-style housewife model.

Splitting also occurs where society insists on the maintenance of rigid social codes inappropriate to changing times and needs, and enforces its demands with techniques of shaming or disapproval (Laing, 1960; Lynd, 1958). A further distinction must be made between Western countries – where rapid social change has been generated within their own traditions – and countries such as India and Japan, where ancient indigenous cultures have been confronted, occupied, and either stimulated or forced to change by societies operating from a totally different cultural frame of reference. Enormous splitting is present in urban-dwellers in these two countries, who may identify with highly conflicting value systems and roles. Such splits, however, may also become a spur to new levels of integration in the unusual individual.

If one major dimension of splitting is generated by rapid social change, the other is related to the childhood splits in the self. This also presents several different aspects. Where parents are unable to relate to their child as an individual – often due to rigid social expectations of their own strong narcissistic needs – a split develops between the true self of the child and the necessity for presenting a false self (Winnicott, 1965). This false self may then substitute for the realization of the truer needs and feelings of the individual, resulting in pervasive social facades, and foreclosing any genuine self-fulfillment. When the usual conscious splitting between social facades appropriate to a variety of roles and the inner self dissipates into unconsciously compulsive and pervasive role playing, then a gaping cleavage is present in the self, a major Pirandellian concern.

Related to the true-self–false-self dichotomy is deeply wounded narcissism with its desperate compensatory mechanisms. The mother who lacks empathy, who is so self-preoccupied as to be unable to retain any strong inner image of the child, or who develops rejecting, sadistic attitudes toward the child, fosters intense feelings of worthlessness and greatly depreciated self-images (Kohut, 1971, 1977, 1984). The child desperately compensates for the lack of self-worth with a number of narcissistic maneuvers in order to restore a modicum of self-esteem, maneuvers which often prove to be ultimately self-destructive. Narcissistic compensations are highly relevant to *Six Characters* and *Henry IV*, and will be delineated below in a variety of specific instances. Particularly relevant is the creation of an idealized self (Kohut, 1971, 1977), which is gradually implemented by roles around which an adult identity crystallizes (Schachtel, 1961). Such idealized role identities, while allowing a modicum of self-worth, ultimately destroy the possibility of genuine fulfillment of adult needs in a variety of relationships.

Attendant upon many if not most instances of intense narcissistic hurt are masochism and depression (Overby and Freudenberger, 1969). Masochism in this form is the idealized hope of gaining love from a rejecting and/or sadistic parent by becoming one day lovable. The quest is futile and the masochist unwittingly seeks out love partners all too similar to the only ones he had known. When deprivation is even greater, illusory hope yields to the despair of depression.

Still another major process of splitting relates to childhood needs to preserve good aspects of the self and of parental imagoes, and to get rid of all the bad images. This often results in adult role relationships in which others are often sharply split into idealized or denigrated figures either all good or all bad (Kernberg, 1975). When this type of splitting becomes involved in group phenomena, a destructive process involving the "ins" and "outs" occurs, with considerable projection of all that is bad onto the "outs."

Although this summary of splitting as related to identity and the self is of necessity a sparse one, it nevertheless focuses on the inner life of the individual. Otherwise, we are left with the alternative of sociologies in which masks and roles are seen as completely constituting the self, and the individual's unique humanity disappears.

We may now be in a position to apply some of our considerations to an analysis of the play. The central metaphor of the work is the search by the six characters for an author, or more properly, their quest for existence. The central paradox is a simple yet profound one: while these creatures of the imagination are more "real" than so-called real people, they remain nonetheless thoroughly dependent on the latter for their embodiment. Without the author, or in his stead, the manager and his actors, there can be no existence. Moreover, the author and subsequently the theater manager are the ones who by the end of the play actually reject them, a rejection that is carried one step further in their repudiation by the actors themselves. For when the actors finally do determine to bring the six characters to actualization, the situation turns into so obvious a farce that the characters in turn repudiate the actors.

What then is the meaning underlying the metaphor, and how is the central paradox to be resolved? In our view, the metaphor is primarily a symbol for modern society in which the sociocultural contexts – as products of rapid social change, disjointedness, and the disintegration characteristic of many industrial, technological, and urban societies – interfere in any number of ways with the ability of the inner self to realize itself through an identity integrated with meaningful social roles and value systems.

To exist, to have an identity is to participate in meaningful relationships. In fact, the dominant metaphor of the play, as we have seen, rests upon repudiation – which we interpret as symbolizing repudiation in the modern world of meaningful self-realization. The author, for example, impotent and unable to embody his characters, concludes by disowning them; this is reflected in the Manager's and Father's impotence in their own roles. The author thus becomes a metaphor for the inability of the creative self to achieve self-realization.

A speech by the Son in Act III suggests, however, that the author's disowning of his characters is due to more than mere impotence. With its rigid and outworn conventions, the theater, understood as a metaphor for society, is unable to tolerate and accept deeper manifestations of the inner self; thus, the author is impelled to withhold his creations just as the Son is impelled throughout the play to withhold himself from involvement with others. The conception of the author then as simply impotent or withholding is far too limited an interpretation of his true role. With his power to create the author holds the tools which allow him to portray not only the human condition but the human impasse as well. He thus becomes an alienist or therapist, in the sense Ben Nelson (1968) uses the terms in discussing the absurdist playwrights.

On a manifest level, the attempt by the actors to enact the roles of the six characters describes the impossibility of entering into genuine communication with the inner self of another. On another level, the play's comic incongruity reveals the enormous split between modern man's role-playing facade – represented appropriately enough by the actors as players – and his inner, truer self – symbolized by the six characters. The divorce between social facade and inner self is further evinced by the Son's distaste when the actors too closely approach to observe him during Act III; he accuses them of "freezing" his image. Here, social role is portrayed as a Procrustean Bed for whatever of the self's inner urges lie concealed within. That not a single three-dimensional character appears in the play is perfectly consonant with its vision of modern man as a fundamentally unrealized being. In this regard, *Six Characters* anticipates the later work of Beckett and other absurdists, obsessed by what they perceive as modern man's nearly total loss of self.

Splitting is further conveyed to the audience by Pirandello's use of humor, briefly alluded to above, and his highly original manipulation of audience response. Alienation and identification, as audience response, occur as the actors – and particularly the six characters – successively demonstrate both intense involvement and subsequent dissociation from their roles; where involvement creates a dramatic situation, dissociation allows its analysis and examination. Concomitantly, the audience's initial identification with the actors is suddenly interrupted and its involvement suspended. The use of this device produces a feeling of being split, thus inducing in the audience a psychic response consonant with the play's meaning and content.

The play's humor depends principally on the juxtaposition of incongruous elements. As such, it represents the fundamental mode by which the split between social role and inner self is dramatically conveyed. Indeed, one could go so far as to assert that an important reason for the play's artistic success is its use of humor to convey what is expressed philosophically and psychologically as an essentially tragic situation. The theme of splitting of the self is clearly developed in the dialogue, and especially in those speeches where the Father dramatically confronts the Manager with the illusoriness of his existence, or where he discusses the mutability of time or where he ultimately challenges the Manager to tell him whether he really knows who he is.

Before we examine the inner drama of the six characters both in terms of more profound psychological levels of meaning and as it relates to the central metaphors and paradoxes of the play, it would be well to reiterate our previously stated position which insists that *the psycho-analytic approach must operate within the larger context of a work's artistic framework and not vice versa*. In a somewhat analogous fashion, dreams are analyzed as they relate to the specific contexts of the therapeutic experience and overall life situation rather than as isolated phenomena as described in Chapter 3. The task of the investigator is to see to what extent meanings underlying the inner drama of the six characters correlate or clash with the central dramatic metaphors and paradoxes, neither severing the inner drama from the total play nor extrapolating meaning exclusively from the inner drama as attempted by the psychoanalyst-critic (Jacobs, 1974; Kligerman, 1962; Wangh, 1976).

In analyzing primary-process material, such as the inner plot, each of the characters as well as their interrelationships must be viewed as fragments of a single psyche, or more correctly, of a state of mind subjected to splitting as a displacement process, in keeping with our first definition. Further, the sequence of the inner drama must be examined in terms of its underlying meaning. We would note, in particular, that only two phases of the overall drama are actually presented, and that it is around these two incidents that the ensuing dramatic action centers. The first of these episodes is the scene at Madame Pace's where the Father goes to have sex with a "poor girl of refined family" (Pirandello, 1952), and is only prevented from doing so when the Mother surprises him with the Stepdaughter and intervenes. The second episode is the fountain scene at the Father's house, where the Son rejects the Mother, the Child drowns, and the Boy shoots himself. The rest of the drama is narrated, but in such a way that the psychological relativism of individual viewpoints is made self-evident.

An examination of the inner drama reveals the presence of traditional Freudian themes. By way of example, we need only cite the Father's incestuous feelings toward the Stepdaughter, the murderous impulses experienced by the play's younger siblings toward one another, and the attendant feelings of guilt, anguish, and remorse – all discussed by Kligerman. Nevertheless, we would suggest that a close examination of the inner drama's key episodes discloses underlying themes of repudiation and deprivation.[5] The audience first becomes aware of their presence in the Father's repudiation of the Mother, sending her off with his former employee. Her departure, however, is perceived by the Son as abandonment reflecting an earlier abandonment when he had been banished by the Father to the countryside as an infant. From the start, the relationship between Father and Stepdaughter is strongly marked by deprivation. Loneliness and emptiness impel him to follow her near her school. His later visit to Madame Pace's, the scene of incestuous sexuality, is clearly brought forth by his sense of being unloved and unlovable to women.

FATHER: ... Ah! what misery, what wretchedness is that of the man who is alone and disdains debasing liaisons! Not old enough to do without women, and not young enough to go and look for one without shame. Misery? It's worse than misery; it's a horror; for no woman can any longer give him love; and when a man feels this ...

(Pirandello, *Six Characters*, p. 229)

Deprivation here is expressed antithetically in terms of the conflict experienced by the Father: against his acute feelings of loneliness is posed his need for human contact, and his attempt to resolve the conflict unwittingly ensnares him into a fundamentally incestuous relationship. Moreover, when confronted and cross-examined by the Manager, the Stepdaughter readily admits that her complaint against the Father is not his desire to have sex with her but his implicit abandonment of the family long before.

STEPDAUGHTER: For one who has gone wrong, sir, he who was responsible for the first fault is responsible for all that follows. *He is responsible for my faults, was, even before I was born. Look at him, and see if it isn't true!*

(Ibid, p. 259) [my italics]

In view of this new interpretive framework, Bentley's contention that the Father's philosophizing merely functions as a schizophrenic defense against being overwhelmed and deluged by the world becomes untenable. Concomitantly, we reject as our only alternative the argument that speech must be interpreted on a purely philosophical level. Rather, we prefer to view the content of the Father's musings on the split nature of the human psyche as being consonant and integral to the structure of the dramatic action. His persistent self-justification and his suffering, in this view, would be interpreted as compensations for damaged narcissism or low self-esteem resulting from rejection and deprivation. From this perspective, the Father may be readily seen to depict in his own person only certain aspects of an entire psychic spectrum which is represented by the six characters and their story in toto, rather than by the in-depth characterization of any single dramatis persona. Applying the concept of the defensive splitting of characters, the Father, as a more central dramatic character, evinces the more acceptable emotions of anguish, guilt, self-justification, and remorse; while the Son, a more subsidiary character, displays a punitive detachment from the Mother and others, and the Boy, who plays no part at all till the end, implicitly manifests murderous rage with its attendant guilt.

Deeply wounded narcissism is reflected in other patterns of response in both Father and Son. The Father's behavior, for instance, in sending off his wife after noting some unspoken attachment on her part, is paradigmatic of one kind of narcissistic compensation resulting from a state of deprivation: "If I can't have everything, I shall take nothing," he seems to say. Similarly, the Son's persistent aloofness is an attempt to punish his Mother, and, as such, is another typical narcissistic compensation against fears of renewed rejection. "Since you rejected me once, I shall continue to punish you for the rest of my life regardless of what you now have to offer me."

The progression of thematic material from the scene with the Stepdaughter to the last episode by the fountain, which as Kligerman points out marks a regression from Oedipal incest material to pre-Oedipal themes of sibling murder and guilt, suggests even more directly the theme of deprivation and accompanying murderous feelings. The normal wish to do away with younger siblings in order to enjoy the exclusive love and attention of the parents is greatly intensified when the parents themselves are emotionally depriving. It is interesting here to note that as deeper and more unacceptable feelings are allowed to emerge, the protagonist is no longer the Father, but either the Son or the Boy. The Father experiences anguish, suffering, and loneliness, but not rage. The Son, on the other hand, through his unusual detachment and withdrawal, implicitly reveals his avoidance of precisely those deep-seated feelings of rage. However, the dramatic material also portrays the

Son's disdainful and angry rejection of his younger half-sisters and brother as well as his rejection and punishment of the Mother for her abandonment of him and for bringing sibling rivals into the world. Here, then, splitting by displacement would appear to assume a defensive function. A similar kind of displacement mechanism is clearly operative in the Child's implicit murder by the Boy who stands by and in no way attempts to save the younger sister from drowning. The Boy's subsequent suicide then may be viewed as giving utterance to the guilt he harbors over his murderous impulses. The inner drama closes as the Son, Father, and Mother draw together anew, now that the two youngest children have been permanently disposed of and the Stepdaughter has run off. Thus, rather than simply depicting, as Wangh (1976) has speculated, aspects of a long-buried Oedipal relationship, the play's inner drama expresses a basic wish to eliminate the three younger siblings.

Rather than now relating the meanings underlying the play's inner drama to events and relationships in Pirandello's life – as Kligerman did in a paradigmatic application of psychoanalysis[6] – our objective is to examine the manner in which such meanings can be effectively integrated into an analysis of the total play. We turn to Norman Holland's (1968) valuable notion that every valid literary work is constructed upon an underlying emotional fantasy which evokes a deep personal response in the audience. But while Holland confines these fantasies to those characteristic of the various psychosexual stages of early childhood, we would expand the scope of his theory to include those emotional states deriving from the internalization of early childhood experiences, and in particular, from close family relationships.

For us, the inner drama of the six characters is ultimately concerned with the most primal form of repudiation a human being can experience, the repudiation of a child by his mother and all the pain attendant upon such a rejection. The young child's identity, self-worth, and very existence depend almost totally upon his or her enjoyment of a reciprocal relationship with the mother. As Winnicott (1965) cogently puts it, it is impossible to speak of the infant alone, but only of the infant and mothering figure. This theme is echoed throughout Pirandello's hall of mirrors and is rejoined by echoes of similar themes of a more properly philosophical and artistic nature. In this regard, we have already discussed the repudiation of the inner self by modern society as well as the artist's rejection of overly rigid theatrical conventions that would become a Procrustean Bed for his creative impulses.[7] On all three levels, however, the individual experiences the loss of a firm social context through which he can establish his slowly unfolding identity. We contend that the theme of repudiation, narcissistic injury, and deprivation pervading the inner drama charges the play's other levels with intense emotion. This emotion evokes a deeper, more personal response on the part of the audience than any of the work's other dramatic elements and devices, of which it is the underlying focus. The successive stages of emotional arousal and frustration experienced by the audience, as remarked by Wangh (1976), and deriving from the play's ambiguous structure and ending, may be viewed as still another form of deprivation consistent with the play's overall technique. To our way of thinking, Pirandello's use of the inner drama reflects his ability to mold past experience and inner conflict into metaphoric expression designed to further his own artistic vision rather than to produce the necessary catharsis predicated by applied psychoanalysis.[8] Thus, the fully integrated valences of Pirandello's hall of mirrors – its reflection of the plights of the child, modern man, and the artist himself – is a many-figured tableau where psychological content and dramatic form and structure continue to reinforce and illumine one another.

HENRY IV

Written directly after publication of *Six Characters* and generally regarded as Pirandello's second great work, *Henry IV* directly confronts the theme of madness. Are Eric Bentley (1966) and Martin Wangh (1976) correct in assuming that madness, masochism, and jealous rage are indeed the boundaries of Pirandello's vision in a limited tragicomedy? Or again, does this awesome drama deal with yet another facet of modern man's desperate but frustrated yearning for self-fulfillment? Given the complexity of the plot, a brief synopsis may be the necessary premise to any analysis of the work.

Where in *Six Characters* we found a constant juxtaposition within the present of the six characters and members of the acting company, *Henry IV*, on the other hand, constantly juxtaposes past and present time. The play moves backwards in time from the present into the medieval past of the German court of the Emperor Henry IV while the characters alternately enact the roles of present and past existences. This juxtaposition has come about accidentally some twenty years prior to the drama's present context when an unnamed individual, participating in a masquerade as the Emperor Henry IV of Germany, took an unwitting tumble from his horse, bumped his head on a rock, and became consequently mad. He had assumed this disguise, we are told, because the woman who was the current object of his affections, the Marchioness Matilda of Spina, and who at the time had rejected his love, had assumed the masquerade role of the Marchioness Matilda of Tuscany. The particular form of madness assumed by the protagonist consists in his deeply rooted belief that he is indeed the Emperor Henry IV, that he is frozen into Henry's twenty-sixth year of life despite the passing of time.

To comfort and succor her mad brother, a wealthy sister of the protagonist decides to redo her solitary Italian villa as a medieval German court. She hires people to serve as courtiers, including four men who will play the important roles of Henry's counselors, and she has them all richly and appropriately costumed for the occasion. The one incongruous element of the latter-day court, but central to the play as dramatic device and metaphor, consists of two large contemporary portraits of the unnamed man and the Marchioness Matilda, outfitted as Henry IV and the Marchioness of Tuscany, which had been painted twenty years before at the time of the masquerade.

Henry is now 50 years old. The dramatic action is precipitated by the sister's death a month previously, and her dying words to her son, Charles Di Nolli, begging him to leave no stone unturned in his efforts to bring his uncle back to sanity. She herself thinks she has discerned signs of recovery. Di Nolli, faithful to his mother's last wishes, calls in a Dr. Genoni to perform the cure. The doctor, an alienist or psychiatrist, devises a remarkable type of shock therapy. He invites to the scene the heroine of the past masquerade, the Marchioness Matilda, together with her daughter, Frida, who is identical to the portrait of her mother done so many years before, and Di Nolli. The daughter and Di Nolli are to enact the past and present images of the Marchioness Matilda of Tuscany and Henry IV, coming alive from within the frames of their portraits, and thereby shocking Henry into an awareness and perception of reality. Also present is the Baron Tito Belcredi, the Marchioness's present lover and most probably a rival to Henry at the time of the masquerade.

The action of the play itself is relatively straightforward. The state of affairs is amusingly conveyed by three present-day Italians, dressed as Henry's counselors, to an utterly confounded neophyte. The "thera-peutic troupe" then arrives. The Marchioness, glimpsing her portrait, is arrested and deeply moved by its frozen image of her youthful self and its uncanny resemblance to her daughter, Frida. For their meeting with Henry, the guests array themselves in medieval dress in different roles of the period. Henry then enters dressed in sackcloth, the sign of his penitence and self-abasement at Canossa. He alternately attacks Belcredi as his enemy, Peter Damian, and expresses tender feelings toward the Marchioness, begging her to free his miserable self transfixed as the 26-year-old Henry. Act I closes as Henry exits leaving the Marchioness deeply moved and overcome with feeling.

Act II opens with a recall of the encounter with Henry, a discussion highlighted by the Marchioness's startling disclosure that she intuitively senses that Henry has indeed recognized her and that the hostility he has demonstrated toward Belcredi springs from discovering the latter to be her lover. In a new exchange between the Marchioness and Henry, the former takes pains to illustrate that, in her historical role no more than in the masquerade of twenty years ago, was the Marchioness as hostile to Henry as he imagines. As soon as they depart, Henry rages to his counselors, irate that the Marchioness should presume to appear there with her lover, clearly revealing his awareness that both counselors and visitors are role-playing in his presence. Nevertheless, despite apparent insight, when the counselors invite him to live in the present, Henry refuses. His unwillingness to do so denotes his reluctance to surrender the role of Emperor and master puppeteer in whose hands lies the power to manipulate the roles of others.

The doctor's stratagem is implemented in Act III. From the frame of the portrait, Frida calls to Henry. Henry initially responds with fears of renewed madness, but these quickly change into violent and passionate calls for revenge at seeing himself the butt of the company's unmerciful ruse. Belcredi, apprised by the counselors of Henry's "sanity" and acting against Genoni's promptings, begins to prod Henry for trifling them and making sport of their quite serious efforts to help him. Henry counters by declaring that for twelve years he had indeed been mad, but that upon recovering, he had perceived that life had passed him by: "... not only had my hair gone grey, but that I was all grey, inside ... I was going to arrive, hungry as a wolf, at a banquet which had already been cleared away ..." (Pirandello, 1952, *Henry IV*, p. 203). His beloved had been taken from him; to return to a world maliciously taunting him as "Henry IV" would have been too painful. The realization of the chasm lying between his unlived life and theirs is profoundly agitating and awakens in him the yearning to possess the Marchioness as she had been, in the image of her daughter, Frida. The climax of the play follows swiftly as Henry embraces Frida, ordering the counselors to seize the others – an order which the counselors much to their amazement proceed to carry out. Belcredi then breaks loose begging Henry to "leave her alone," exclaiming that he, Henry, is "no madman." "I'm not mad, eh!" (ibid., p. 207) retorts Henry, drawing his sword and plunging it into Belcredi. Continuing to taunt Henry, Belcredi, fatally wounded, is borne offstage by the others. Henry then summons his counselors and standing like a wise man in their midst, utters the play's closing lines, transfixed forever in the role of the Emperor Henry IV.

It is our contention that *Henry IV*, like *Six Characters*, responds to an artistic vision considerably broader than either Bentley or Wangh envisaged with their emphasis on psychopathology. The play's structural aspects disclose more profound, extensive levels of meaning which must be integrated with precisely the themes of madness, masochism, deprivation, and jealousy analyzed in their respective essays.

Henry IV, like *Six Characters*, is shaped in a naturalistic mold. Similar to the earlier play as well is the juxtaposition of two sets of characters. In *Six Characters*, however, spatial dimensions and characterization are juxtaposed within a contemporary time scheme. In very different fashion, the characters in the later play are juxtaposed in their changing roles across a diachronic time scheme, rapidly moving from the present to a remote historical past, thence to twenty and finally to eight years prior to the dramatic action. That the themes of *Henry IV* can be expressed as jealousy, insanity, masochism, and deprivation should not alter the fundamental consideration that these themes are depicted within thoroughly unique temporal and role structures. The unusual nature of the play's temporal structure is emphasized by the characters' changing names and roles. The young man who at 26 assumed the name and role of Henry IV is known by no other name in the drama, despite the fact that during its second half he exists consciously within the present. His name is only of the role. On the other hand, there are four characters – Frida, Di Nolli, Dr. Genoni, and Belcredi –whose names are only of the present although each plays a role in the past. In the case of the

Marchioness, her first name, Matilda, is the link between the contemporary figure and the historic Matilda of Tuscany. Finally, there are the four counselors each with a double set of names corresponding to the character's historical and present-day identity: Harold/Frank, Landolph/Lolo, Ordulph/Momo, Berthold/Fino. It is inconceivable that Pirandello would have assigned such past, present, or double names to characters completely at whim. It becomes necessary, therefore, to assess the significance of this unusual relationship between time and role, an analysis that can only proceed in conjunction with a basic study of the play's central metaphors and paradoxes. A few comments about how these differ from those of *Six Characters* are also pertinent.

The paradox that "life-in-theater" is "theater-in-life" is transformed in *Henry IV* into "life-of-madness" is "madness-of-life." When the two (Pirandello) plays are compared, the later one appears rather close to the Laingian (1965) view of sanity-in-madness and madness-in-sanity. The play's central metaphor is the portrait, the image that captures, freezes, and evokes in us the feelings of a past self. The metaphor anticipates the structural development of the drama: an unknown individual is frozen, first by tragic accident and then by psychological necessity, into an old self, or more precisely, into an idealized, grandiose image of that past self at the same time he is unable to fulfill the yearnings and needs of his real self, and half-mad, half-sane, he lives on until one last tragedy freezes him forever into the portrait of his past.

The Doctor explains the significance of a portrait as the reflection of a past self.

DOCTOR: Quite right! Because a portrait is always there fixed in the twinkling of an eye: for the young lady something far away and without memories, while for the Marchioness, it can bring back everything: movements, gestures, looks, smiles, a whole heap of things.

DONNA MATILDA: Exactly!

(Ibid, p. 152)

A few pages on, Belcredi muses on the relationship between the portrait and Henry, frozen forever into the role of Holy Roman Emperor.

BELCREDI: ... look at him – (points to the portrait) – Ha! a smack on the head, and he never moves again: Henry IV for ever!

(Ibid., p. 159)

An important metaphor in *Six Characters*, that of role-playing as theater, becomes transformed in *Henry IV* into the masquerade or the wearing of masks in life. Pirandello uses this metaphor to portray his perception of the cleavages or splits in the self.

HENRY: ... We're all fixed in good faith in a certain concept of ourselves. However, Monsignor, while you keep yourself in order, holding on with both your hands to your holy habit, there slips down from your sleeves, there peels off from you like ... like a serpent ... something you don't notice: life Monsignor! (Turns to the Marchioness) Has it never happened to you, my Lady, to find a different self in yourself? Have you always been the same? ...

(Ibid., p. 169)

[...]

you, you, my Lady, certainly don't dye your hair to deceive the others, not even yourself; but only to cheat your own image a little before the looking-glass. I do it for a joke! You do it seriously! But I assure you that you too, Madame, are in masquerade, though it be in all seriousness ...

(Ibid., p. 169–70)

The compulsion to don masks is a clear sign of madness, just as the unconscious choice of masquerading through life rather than living it is a clear sign of Laing's madness-in-life. The play's true dramatic conflict, therefore, begins not when Henry tumbles from his horse and awakens unwittingly convinced that he is Henry IV, but rather twelve years later when he realizes that he is *not* the Emperor at all, when his profound needs force him to remain frozen behind a mask of which he is fully conscious. Parenthetically, Henry seems himself aware of some of his life-thwarting needs. When invited by Ordulph to switch on the electric light, he passionately demands his old lamp, clinging to it as to a fate that has already been ordained in history, eschewing the anxiety and chaos of an existence to be lived in the present.

ORDULPH: Well, then shall I turn it on now (the electric light)?

HENRY IV: No, it would blind me! I want my lamp!

(Ibid., p. 193)

[...]

the men of the twentieth century are torturing themselves in ceaseless anxiety to know how their fates and fortunes will work out! Whereas you are already in history with me ... And sad is my lot, hideous as some of the events are, bitter the struggles and troubled the time – still all history! All history that cannot change, understand? All fixed forever!

(Ibid., p. 195)

We are now in a position to relate the play's unusual temporal and role structures to its metaphors and central paradox. The meaning of these structures is clarified if we consider, as we did in our analysis of *Six Characters*, man's profound need to forge an identity through meaningful relationships with others. In dramatic terms, then, the juxtaposition of roles and time sequences conveys Pirandello's belief in the cleavages of the self, *particularly as they reflect the conflict between the individual's yearnings for self-fulfillment and his life-thwarting need to masquerade in various roles.* Henry IV, known in the play only as Henry IV, illustrates madness as a life frozen into his mask. He stands in contrast to the others, particularly the "therapeutic troupe," who masquerade wildly through life dissipating all chance of self-fulfillment. When Henry regains awareness twelve years after his initial fall, his need to persevere in masquerade allows us to perceive that his only context for identity is to abide as Henry IV.

The Marchioness Matilda, as her single name implies, is remarkably similar in all three of her past, present, and historical roles, demonstrating throughout her ambivalent rejection and sympathy for Henry. The last group of characters – Dr. Genoni, Frida, Charles Di Nolli, and Tito Belcredi – play their historical roles clumsily; they are clearly rooted in the present. In fact, the function of this last group is rather similar to that of the professional actors in Pirandello's earlier play whose inept attempts to fill the roles of the six characters underscore even more markedly the split between self and role. Finally, we must consider Henry's philosophy, which in our view is fully consonant with the dramatic depiction of splits in the self, and the conflict between self-actualization and the need for masks. The latter emerges in a number of speeches, particularly the one where he mentions the Irish priest brimming with life as he dreams but who upon awakening reverts to the mask of the zealous and stodgy clergyman.

HENRY IV: ... Look here, doctor! I remember a priest, certainly Irish, a
nice-looking priest, who was sleeping in the sun one
November day, with his arm on the corner of the bench
of a public garden. He was lost in the golden delight of the
mild sunny air which must have seemed for him almost
summery. One may be sure that in that moment he did not
know any more that he was a priest, or even where he was.
He was dreaming ... A little boy passed with a flower in his
hand. He touched the priest with it here on the neck. I saw
him open his laughing eyes, while all his mouth smiled with
the beauty of his dream. He was forgetful of everything ...
But all at once, he pulled himself together, and stretched out
his priest's cassock and there came back to his eyes the same
seriousness which you have seen in mine: because the Irish
priests defend the seriousness of their Catholic faith with the
same zeal with which I defend the sacred rights of hereditary
monarchy!

(Ibid., p. 206)

In this connection, we would also remark about the allusion to
prostitutes who sleep with Henry under the guise of being his wife and
who burst into strident laughter when he calls them Bertha of Susa: in
bed, naked, we can throw off our masks.[9] Thus, a remarkable similarity
of theme can be discerned in both *Henry IV* and *Six Characters. However,
where underlying meaning in the latter was focused on the impossibility of the
inner self to find realization within a social context, Henry IV hinges upon the
tragic assumption of masks in social roles, masks which ultimately destroy any
chance for inner realization.* As in *Six Characters*, the reader stands in the
same hall of mirrors where diverse aspects of the self and its splits are
reflected endlessly back and forth. Or perhaps the image is rather that of
a many-faceted gem that we turn over and over in the palm of our hand
to examine. Pirandello's exploration of the human psyche in *Henry IV*
leads him to the threshold of modern man's profoundly existential
dilemma: his need for masks even at the price of his own self-
fulfillment.

In assessing Pirandello's exploration of the modern dilemma of the
self, we must indicate another formal aspect of *Henry IV*, one which
differs sharply from the earlier play: the presence of three-dimensional
characters rather than the exclusively one- and two-dimensional figures
of *Six Characters*. With this important difference in mind, we can now

examine character interaction and characterization, particularly as they relate to Henry. *Rather than elucidate Henry's psychopathology alone, our task will essentially be to investigate the relationship between character and the existential conflict over man's self-fulfillment.*

The true drama of Henry's madness is the paradox of his need to masquerade, however conscious he may be of its fictive character and however destructive and unfulfilling his role. Wounded narcissism, masochism, and deprivation – those haunting specters of childhood pain – together with man's profoundly universal need for an identity, drive Henry on to his final destruction. Even the Oedipal rivalry and jealousy experienced by Henry toward Belcredi are colored by rejection (by the Marchioness), deprivation, and repudiation (the same constellation of themes present in *Six Characters*, where they appear reinforced by the Father's search for the Stepdaughter). Thus Henry's reaction to regaining awareness of his old self is filled with imagery of deprivation.

HENRY IV: Not only had my hair gone grey, but that I was all grey inside . . . I was going to arrive, hungry as a wolf, at a banquet which had already been cleared away.

(Ibid., p. 203)

We may even speculate that Henry's rejection at the hands of the Marchioness twenty years before is by implication merely a repetition of a still earlier maternal rejection. For Henry is portrayed as a man of deep inner coldness, or in more properly psychoanalytic language, as a man without a warm maternal internalization or presence.

BELCREDI: . . . Evidently, because that immediate lucidity that comes from acting, assuming a part, at once put him out of key with his own feelings, which seemed to him not exactly feelings, but like something he was obliged to give the value there and then of – what shall I say – of an act of intelligence, to make up for that sincere cordial warmth he felt lacking. So he improvised, exaggerated, let himself go, so as to distract and forget himself. He appeared inconstant, fatuous, and – yes – even ridiculous sometimes.

(Ibid., pp. 157–8)

That Henry was attracted to a woman seemingly incapable of loving him indicates the extent to which masochism forms an integral part of his personality. But it is masochism motivated by what contemporary psychoanalytic thinking posits as the child's urgent need to sustain at all costs, with a rejecting, neglectful, or sadistic mother, a love relationship that at best is extremely tenuous (Menaker, 1953). Unless he or she can achieve this, the child faces a life of utter deprivation and futility, a life of despair and depression. Later, as an adult, he is unconsciously drawn to similar masochistic love relationships because he inwardly experiences such relationships as being the only ones he is capable of having. His self-abasement obscures the true nature of the rejecting love object and affords some small hope that if he can but himself change, the other will then love him.

In view of Henry's masochistic relationship with the Marchioness, it is hardly accidental that Pirandello should freeze his protagonist into the role of Henry IV during the latter's twenty-sixth year. This is the time, we will recall, when in order to rescind his excommunication and to prevent his being deposed by the Imperial electors, he had been forced to abase himself before both Marchioness and Pope. For had Henry not humiliated himself before the temporal and spiritual powers of the eleventh century at this time, existence would have stretched before him, a terrible void of nothingness. Masochism of this kind also tinges the relationship between Belcredi and the Marchioness, although it functions there as a lesser motif reflecting what is in Henry a dominant theme.

However important the function of rejection, deprivation, and masochism as psychic determinants of Henry's personality, his actions as a dramatic character yet proceed from quite another though related source. To us it seems quite evident that they are motivated by Henry's profoundly wounded narcissism – another familiar theme from *Six Characters*. As noted earlier, against this wounded narcissism or painfully low self-esteem, the individual contrives a system of compensatory defenses intended to make his life at least minimally endurable. Henry's major defense is clearly the implementation of a grandiose, idealized self-image into an adult role-identity, thus foreclosing fulfillment of any genuine needs for human closeness.

While most of the play's dramatic action is contingent upon the fanciful scheme devised by Dr. Genoni, there are in fact three events which occur without apparent premeditation. The first such incident occurs in Act II as Henry, in high fury, reveals his awareness of the doctor's ruse by disclosing the real identities of the Marchioness and her lover. The other two incidents occur during Act III; the first, when

Belcredi mocks Henry for trifling with the company despite their having taken their parts quite seriously; and the second at the end of the play when Henry, after seizing Frida, and instigated by Belcredi's taunting accusations that he is not mad at all, becomes a murderer. In all these instances, the fundamental motivation must be understood as originating in the need to recompense profoundly wounded narcissism.

Let us examine the first of these three incidents. A closer look reveals that paradoxically Henry confesses his awareness of his surroundings not at the time of any new rejection by the Marchioness, but just at the point when Matilda demonstrates affectionate and sympathetic feelings toward him.

DONNA MATILDA: ... (looks at him; then very softly as if in confidence) You love her still [Matilda of Tuscany, but referring to herself]?

HENRY IV: (puzzled) Still? Still, you say? You know, then. But nobody knows! Nobody must know!

DONNA MATILDA: But perhaps she knows, if she has begged so hard for you.

(Ibid., p. 187)

The reason for Henry's apparently bizarre reaction lies in his adoption of one of the most self-destructive forms of defense against wounded narcissism – a mechanism one desperately clings to in order to prevent any further painful disappointment after severe rejection and deprivation have already occurred. "If I can't have everything, I'll take nothing," is the paradigm on which this kind of defense is modeled. Already present in the Father in *Six Characters*, it sounds a more dominant chord in *Henry IV*. Needless to say, so desperate a measure to preserve one's self-esteem ultimately leaves the individual completely empty-handed. Turning to the last scene, Henry's actions are clearly motivated by a last attempt *to preserve the final vestiges of a narcissistic compensation for feelings of utter worthlessness.*

HENRY IV: (remains apart, peering at one and now at the other under the accusation and the mockery of what all believe to be a cruel joke of his, which is now revealed. He has shown by the flashing of his eyes that he is meditating a revenge ...).

BELCREDI: We've had enough of this joke now.

HENRY IV: Who said joke?

DOCTOR: (loudly to Belcredi) Don't excite him, for the love of God!

BELCREDI: (without lending an ear to him, but speaking louder) But they have said so (pointing to the four young men), they, they!

HENRY IV: (turning around and looking at them) You? Did you say it was all a joke?

(Ibid., p. 200)

[...]

HENRY IV: All by itself, who know how, one day the trouble here (touches his forehead) mended ... Ah! – then as he says (alludes to Belcredi) away, away with this masquerade, this incubus! Let's open the windows, life once again! Away! Away! Let's run out! (Suddenly pulling himself up) But where? And to do what? To show myself to all, secretly as Henry IV, not like this, but arm in arm with you among my dear friends.

(Ibid., pp. 202–3)

Already Henry has confessed that even eight years ago he was afraid to venture into the world for fear of the ridicule that would greet him. With these words, he reveals the extreme and continuing fragility of the compensatory mechanism.

One final issue of central importance is how to integrate our analysis of Henry's narcissism with the play's overall artistic vision. Expressed otherwise, how are we to reconcile wounded narcissism with the need to masquerade in roles that sever and truncate our lives and keep us from achieving self-fulfillment? In *Henry IV*, the need to don masks and to structure one's entire existence around an assumed role is perceived by the author as a response to narcissistic wounds sustained again and again. *In lives where relationships affording meaningful existence and identity to the individual are lacking; where love relationships with mother and family and later lovers and friends are extremely tenuous; where relationships in work and community are impersonal and removed, where the individual experiences life as inner emptiness and himself as worthless, a semblance of self and self-worth are achieved by masquerading in various roles.*

But at what cost to his fragile humanity does man sustain this vicarious mode of living?

Thus we find that *Henry IV*'s unusual temporal and role structures, its metaphors and central paradox, can be fully integrated with the work's three-dimensional characterization and philosophy. What emerges is a unified artistic vision, a message at once powerful and tragic for modern man. Its intuitive grasp of his need to yield to self-destruction through masquerade and self-deception surely anticipates by decades similar conclusions of an empirical, scientific nature. *Henry IV* performs the magical feat so often noted by Freud (1908): it reveals the vision that mysteriously crystallizes in the mind of the poet.

NOTES

1. The second discussant at the New York Psychoanalytic Institute Meeting was Martin Bergmann, but he spoke from notes, and his remarks have not been made available.
2. See Norman Holland (1968) and Gilbert Rose (1980) for a more comprehensive exposition of this point of view.
3. As it pertains to drama, an acceptable formulation of the term "grotesque" is the one suggested by the Polish critic, Jan Kott (1964, p. 141): "This dispute about the tragic and grotesque interpretations of human fate reflects the everlasting conflict of two philosophies and two ways of thinking; of two opposing attitudes defined by the Polish philosopher, Leszek Koakowski, as the irreconcilable antagonism between the priest and the clown. Between tragedy and grotesque there is the same conflict for or against such notions as eschatology, belief in the absolute, hope for the ultimate solution of the contradiction between the moral order and every-day practice. Tragedy is the theatre of priests, grotesque is the theatre of clowns."
4. See Leon Edel (1969) for a similar approach.
5. Important aspects of our analysis reflect more closely Jacob's rather than Kligerman's or Wangh's views. Our thesis assumes an expanded conceptualization of primary-process functioning as delineated in Chapters 3 and 4.
6. Kligerman (1962) correlated dramatic actions with biographical events such as the incestuous theme between Father and Stepdaughter in *Six Characters* with Pirandello's over-attachment to his own daughter and the discovery scene at Madame Pace's with the confrontation of Pirandello's father in an affair.
7. By having the *Rules of the Game* – a naturalistic-type drama in rehearsal at the beginning of *Six Characters* – replaced by this new open-structured play of the six characters, Pirandello suggests that he would defy and prevail over long-established theatrical conventions.
8. The assumption that the artist creates to have a necessary catharsis is common in applied psychoanalysis, and is incorporated into Kligerman's essay, "A psycho-analytic study of *Six Characters*."
9. This allusion to Henry's use of prostitutes reiterates one of the earlier play's central motifs; the meeting of the Father and Stepdaughter at the small-town bordello where he is a well-known client. The theme of prostitution in both works is used

in part to highlight the male protagonists' incapacity to sustain a true love relationship with one woman; it is also used to provide a dramatic context in which the individual's masks may be torn away: thus, in *Six Characters* the Father's secret jaunts to the bordello are exposed, while in *Henry IV*, the prostitutes jeer at the entire masquerade.

8

Pinter's *Homecoming*: Imagoes in Dramatic Action

THE HOMECOMING

Harold Pinter is now acclaimed to be among the most exciting of contemporary playwrights and *The Homecoming* perhaps the most provocative of his plays. Reams have been written about his works, particularly about *The Homecoming*. But the question still remains, what are they all about? "Enthrallingly dramatic while remaining exasperatingly obscure," a comment by a daily reviewer, sums up the general reactions of drama critics and audiences. On a more sophisticated level, Elizabeth Hardwick (1967) of *The New York Review* points out, "It is characteristic of these plays that they are not symbolic or distorted; they are instead prosaic, recognizable, but unexplained." Even the comments on Pinter's style and dialogue are paradoxical: Martin Esslin (1961, 1971) and Elizabeth Hardwick indicate Pinter's extraordinary gift for naturalistic lower-class dialogue, while Kelly Morris (1966) and Richard Schechner (1966) emphasize Pinter's refusal to reveal information: "We expect to discover what it's all about. Pinter intentionally disappoints this expectation and leaves his audience anxiously confused." Michael Smith of *The Village Voice* (April 1965) puts it in a nutshell: "The dialogue is both accurate and improbable." Characterization is couched in equally incongruous statements: Martin Esslin and Richard Schechner stress the characters' lack of identity, background, and motivation, while other critics like Elizabeth Hardwick express how profoundly real they are.

How are these paradoxes to be resolved? Pinter's plays are Janus-faced, pointing toward not only the characters' relationships to each other, but also their inner dynamics, the outside and inside combined through dramatic images of the seemingly commonplace. His dramas start in a traditional, naturalistic way, usually involving the advent and impact of a visitor – a metaphor that will be explored later. But the action then proceeds on what seems to be an increasingly absurd or surrealistic note, with foreboding and dread. Dramatically, the plays not only always move from the inner psychic reality of the characters, as in traditional drama; but they also actually portray psychic reality directly, the projections of internalized image-relationships from the childhood of the various characters. In this, Pinter departs from traditional drama and joins company with those modern playwrights beginning with Pirandello who emphasize psychological processes. Thus, in *The Homecoming* Pinter is actually able to portray simultaneously social relationship and psychic reality, offering a dramatic experience rich in ambiguity. His locus of consciousness is the crossroads where past internalized familial images of the psyche interpenetrate social role and relationship.

To apprehend the ambiguity, the viewer must attend to the plays flexibly, to remain on the threshold of rational attention to character interaction while facing inward into old imagoes and emotional fantasies of the psyche itself. Only through such a dual perspective can he recognize the superb clarity and richness of a play like *The Homecoming* and avoid a one-sided viewing that is either too psychological or too socially thematic, which is present in almost all criticism on *The Homecoming*. Thus, the viewer must live in the interstices between the psyche and social reality.

In its portrayal of different levels of reality and their interaction, *The Homecoming* is perhaps the most successful of Pinter's plays. The plot begins on the naturalistic note of a man, a professor of philosophy in the United States, bringing home for the first time his wife, mother of three sons, to his lower-class London family. He is the returning hero, the eldest son who left six years ago and made good. As a man of taste, learning, and refinement, he is almost unrecognizable as a member of the clan, which consists of a father, uncle, and two younger brothers – four men without a woman. The wife and mother, Jessie, is already dead. The action takes place in an enormous room, all masculine in its lack of a woman's touch and expressive of deprivation in its dreary bareness.

Before the arrival of Teddy and his wife, Ruth, Pinter brilliantly portrays the characters of the four men and the relationships among them through dialogue that is primitive and crude. It is back-biting,

jibing, and completely undermining in its competitiveness. It reflects a
family almost devoid of love and barbaric in its desperation. The
milieu, as conceived by Peter Hall, the director, is that of a jungle.
Nevertheless, the men manage to hold together as a family. The
father, Max, an old bully and braggart of 70, tries to dominate the
household as well as to fulfill the missing maternal function of the
cook; but he only succeeds in cowing Sam, his submissive younger
brother of 63. As Max trumpets his status through tales of better days,
Sam still searches for his through his present job as chauffeur. Cut
from the same cloth as that of the old man is the middle son, Lenny –
cynical, taunting, sarcastic, ridiculing, malevolent to Max, in real life a
pimp. Then there is Joey, the dense, good-natured youngest brother –
would-be boxer with little status among the others. The room is
dominated by Max's large chair, with Sam submissively by his side,
Lenny asserting his presence, and Joey content to be outside the family
circle.

A homecoming is a tale often enacted with many variations. Its
effects on the family are often quite unpredictable, not at all what the
returning hero expects. A college student returning home on vacation,
a soldier coming out of service, men and women migrating to other
cities or shores can all testify to this. The familial response, the "gut
reactions," are made of the stuff of past days. The returning hero
becomes almost unrecognizable to himself in the mirror of his family. Is
he the man of his present days, or once again an old self, one seemingly
discarded over past years? As Teddy exclaims and reiterates, "Nothing
has changed!" including himself.

Pinter explores this theme as it is enacted in this particular family.
One does not have to look further for allegory, as several reviewers
have done; the play is understandable without such reference. The
dramatic action is set into motion by Teddy and Ruth's visit. The
family is now complete. Only seemingly absent is the dead wife and
mother, Jessie.

With the advent of Ruth, the action takes an increasing turn to the
absurd or the surreal. From an initial portrayal of shyness in the
beginning, a respectable wife and mother about to meet her in-laws
(and such in-laws) for the first time, Ruth's role suddenly and
inexplicably changes to becoming seductive and infantilizing toward
Lenny. She then becomes involved in increasingly abandoned love-
making with Lenny and Joey in front of her husband's eyes, culminating

in her leaving husband and children for a working arrangement to whore for the father and brothers-in-law. Yet her apparent free-wheeling sexual response to these men, at least as shown in the Peter Hall production, is at complete variance with the totally impersonal and inexpressive manner in which she acts her role.

Ruth is undoubtedly the key to *The Homecoming*. But how is her role to be understood? Various writers have taken different tacks. Some, like Bernard Dukore (1971), claim that, as the action of the play proceeds, Ruth changes from Teddy's wife to mother of the family, replacing Jessie. Other writers, like Augusta Walker (1971) stress Ruth as a real character, whose homecoming to her original environment is more emotionally and sensuously satisfying than her stale life with Teddy in America. Both of these interpretations in themselves still leave the actions in the play in the realm of the absurd, expressed by the dictum enunciated by Walter Kerr and Michael Smith, that with Pinter everything can happen. But Pinter's dramas are in fact the opposite of absurd, for his plays unfold from the taut inner logic of psychic reality.

Ruth's presence is the stone dropped into the middle of the pool, sending out ripples in all directions; a catalyst setting off a chain of reactions in the five men. She revives in the family members the unconscious, living image of the dead wife and mother, Jessie, and their intense relationships to this image, and, in the light of the image, the old relationships to each other. The presence of this new woman in their midst invokes in each of them the old family pattern of five men with one woman, image-relationships that have unconsciously continued inside each of their psyches over the years.

Ruth's roles as wife of Teddy and mother-image to all are like the switch at two railroad tracks, able to send an oncoming train in either of two directions. Her double role is presaged; she is actually the mother of three young sons. As the play progresses, to whatever extent she runs on the track of her own character, she also rides the rails of the others' inner image and fantasy of Jessie. This dual role can be baffling to the onlooker unless it is understood. Hints of this duality occur soon after her appearance, toward the end of the first act, as she subtly reverses roles with Teddy and Lenny. Teddy, the assertive, protective husband advising her to go to sleep while he stays up, ends by bedding down as she goes out for a walk. Lenny's threatening stories of beating up women and his bold advances to her are a thin disguise for his infantile cravings, which are portrayed by Ruth first becoming seductive, then infantilizing, toward him over a glass of water. The first subtle effects of the homecoming are felt: husband and brother-in-law turn into sons. And Ruth becomes both the seductive woman and the men's inner images of the maternal presence. This double role of Ruth as both character and non-character simultaneously is conveyed through the incongruity of her freewheeling sexuality being enacted so impersonally, as if she were equal parts woman and puppet.

The later effects of Ruth's presence are not so subtle. Max progresses from undermining Sam before Ruth to becoming brutal with Joey and Sam, and ends intensely jealous of Ruth's cuddling of the "baby" of the family, Joey, as the curtain closes. It is clearly an image of the jealous husband-father reevoked from the past. Lenny clashes with Teddy by posing a challenging question on philosophy. Teddy one-ups him by declaring that it's not within his province. Their sibling battle is later portrayed in a childhood image of Teddy having eaten Lenny's sandwich. The competition between the males of the family over one woman is increasingly magnified by Ruth's presence.

Ruth receiving the later sexual advances of Joey and Lenny toward her, and then agreeing to whore for them at the instigation of Lenny, albeit in a totally impersonal manner, can be seen in all their incongruity as partially Ruth representing the father's and younger brothers' image of Jessie and their old relationship to her; and as partially Ruth's own search for sensuality and encounter in a homecoming to her old background. In one of Ruth's Janus faces, she becomes a puppet on strings, impersonally dancing to the jerks of each of the men's image of Jessie. To Lenny and Max she is the sexual, seductive woman seen as whore, and acts accordingly. But to Joey, her sexuality is maternal cuddling, and he wants her all to himself. Joey's response, while at first contradictory to Lenny's description of his sexual prowess, is not surprising. For if the image-relationships being enacted are at the same age level as Ruth's children, all under 6 (as Martin Esslin so insightfully noted), then Joey as the youngest would still be craving for maternal warmth. In Ruth's other face, she is the unhappy woman escaping from a secure but desolately unhappy marriage with a coldly detached husband – "It's all rock. And sand. It stretches . . . so far . . . everywhere you look" – into a more sensuous situation where she can demand what she needs and wants. The homecoming thus becomes more truly hers than Teddy's.

Where is Teddy in all of this? Where he was years before. "It's like a urinal. A filthy urinal!" he complains to Ruth, his initial enthusiasm for the homecoming transformed to an urge to flee, just as he had done some six years previously. In the presence of Ruth as maternal image, his battle with Lenny erupts. But Teddy's basic way of slugging it out with the family is by rising above them with an air of superiority, not letting himself be drawn into the mire of their backbiting and brawling. Thus, as Max and the brothers battle and tug over Ruth, Teddy remains coldly aloof, dignified – humorous and absurd on the surface to be sure, but not in the light of his characteristic reaction to the family. Teddy as philosopher epitomizes this attitude:

> It's a question of how far you can operate on things and not in things. You're just objects . . . But you're lost in it. You won't get me being . . . I won't be lost in it.

His leaving by himself is the leaving of six years ago. "Teddy . . . don't become a stranger" is a mother's farewell. Jessie's favorite thus departs again as Ruth in Jessie's image remains loyal to home and hearth, to the men who need her more, and whom she as Ruth needs.

Max's initial mistaking of Ruth for a tart Teddy brought home introduces us to the crucial theme of Jessie as whore. Max unwittingly exclaims, "I've never had a whore under this roof before. Ever since your mother died!" The "slip" is later confirmed in a challenging outburst by Sam (who then faints in submission), who reveals that Jessie was once "had" in the back of his Snipe by Mac, Max's old friend. The theme of whore is enhanced as the play progresses by Ruth becoming increasingly seductive and openly sexual with Lenny and Joey, culminating in a business transaction to whore for the father and brother-in-law. It is a transaction, however, in which Ruth has the upper hand.

How are we to understand the image of Jessie as whore? And how is this related to the image of the play as a jungle, and the metaphor of the visitor? On the naturalistic level, there are the tale of Jessie's promiscuity and the implications of Ruth's being a nude model. In the more psychological realm, Ruth's agreement to whore for the family represents the men's debased childhood image of the mother. But their hostile image of the woman, and competitive attacks on each other, are not only due to Oedipal rivalry, which Martin Esslin (1971) and other critics have so emphasized. Missing from all essays on *The*

Homecoming is the crucial dimension of early maternal deprivation, with its concomitant hostility. Yet the play is actually rife with such images: the bare, dreary living room; Max's initial invitation to Teddy to "cuddle;" Lenny's lambasting of Max as mother substitute (both as cook in the present and as provider in the past, even when Jessie was alive); Teddy stealing and eating Lenny's sandwich – the ultimate attack; Joey wanting only to be cuddled by Ruth. Moreover, the foreboding and dread, so ever present in the play, are far more related from a psychoanalytic standpoint to the hostilities of the early maternal relationship than to the rivalries of the Oedipal period.

This psychological dimension in *The Homecoming*, described by Hall's image of the play as a jungle, is related to Pinter's delineation of the visitor, which touches upon a crucial aspect of social violence. The visitor, Pinter related in an interview, is a metaphor for the dread knock on the door the Jews in Europe expected for so long, which itself became a metaphor for one of the most brutal expressions of social violence in the modern world. In combining this metaphor of social violence with the psychological roots of violence, Pinter brings about a true homecoming by locating both within the family structure of early childhood.

We have emphasized above the unique dramatic dimension in Pinter's *The Homecoming* as the simultaneous portrayal of past internalized familial images of the psyche with social interaction around the theme of violence. We must now ask how this is conveyed dramatically. What devices and techniques does Pinter use to bring about this rich ambiguity? One major way is the initial tantalizing use of naturalism, seemingly followed by increasingly absurd or surrealistic dramatic action, such as Ruth's willingness to whore for the family. One reviewer remarks that Pinter denies the audience every incidental expectation, such as by having people entering and not speaking, and by frequently using non sequiturs. It is by breaking up the "rational possibilities of the moment" (W. Kerr, *New York Herald Tribune*, 1965) while using uncannily realistic speech (Hardwick, 1967) that Pinter jars the audience from the expectably known to a deeper psychic reality that joins together interaction with inner motivation, the facade of behavior with the wellsprings of character. The extraordinary interspersion of silences and the frequent double meanings in the dialogue also contribute importantly to an experience of ambiguity. The characterization of Ruth and the manner in which she is played are an example of how dialogue, action, and style lend themselves to a paradoxical presentation of different levels of reality. Her dialogue and actions by themselves could be expressive of a deeply unhappy and frustrated wife seeking sensuality and contact; but presented in such a totally impersonal and unemotional way they reveal her simultaneously as a noncharacter (the men's image of Jessie) and as Teddy's wife.

Still another major dramatic device is Pinter's use of humor. Incongruity and paradox, the everyday world and the inner one, are the matrices in which humor is constantly created; their repeated use indicates that different levels of reality are operative. Lenny exclaims, "And he didn't go the whole hog," commenting again and again upon Joey's two hours in bed with Ruth, and, to the laughter of the audience, accusing Ruth of being a tease. The humor arising here out of the incongruity of the situation serves not only to entertain but also to convey the infantile relationship of Joey to Jessie, and his old need for cuddling. Similar to this is the transaction of Ruth whoring for Max and Lenny, bargained for in an impeccable business manner: absurdly incongruous and humorous at first glance, but profoundly expressive both of their image of Jessie and of her dominance. Then there is Max's desperately jealous attempt to grab Ruth's love as the play ends, as she pats Joey's head on her knee; a jealous, competitive response of the past but set against the infirmity of an old man. Here, the comic becomes tragicomic in its revelations of reality.

Pinter (1967) insists that he writes realistically:

> I like to create character and follow a situation to its end . . . Each play is quite a different world. The problem is to create a unique world in each case, with a totally different set of characters.

In another interview with Henry Hewes (Hewes, 1967), Pinter remarks, "I am only concerned with this particular family. The whole play happens on a quite realistic level from my point of view." One must state, however, that the play is "realistic" only if one is concerned with the actual portrayal of the inner dynamics of character as these affect relationships, and in this psychological sense Pinter becomes deeply realistic. Further support for this perspective comes from Peter Hall, the director of The Homecoming, in an interview with Samuel Hirsch: "Everything exists on ambivalent levels: hate and love are co-mingled, so are the real and surreal, the rational and irrational ... We worked mainly on the inner life of the characters, their inner motivations."

In summary, *The Homecoming* is Harold Pinter's most complex and profound achievement on the stage. It continues Pinter's brilliant mode of portraying inner psychic reality in the form of past internalized image-relationships of childhood in their interpenetration of social role and relationship in traditional character interactions. This is done in *The Homecoming* through the original dramatic device of a character, Ruth, being both character and non-character simultaneously. By representing in many of Ruth's actions the five men's past images of the dead mother, Jessie, Pinter is able to explore the psychic roots of violence within the family, and by using the metaphor of the visitor, to relate these roots to one of the major examples of social violence of modern times.

THE LOVER

We have elaborated extensively a point of view in understanding *The Homecoming*. It might be of value to ascertain whether the same approach is applicable to Pinter's other plays, and what modifications might have to be made. Perhaps *The Lover* provides the most concise illustration of his thorough exploration into psychological processes. What seems to be an absurd situation and relationship is again a paradoxical expression of psyche and society in a way that is ultrarealistic. Here the inner dynamics of character are again dramatically reenacted rather than merely inferred, as in traditional drama, and again they show their interpenetration into social role.

Pinter takes a very respectable, upper-middle-class couple in their thirties, a financier and his charming wife, who blandly talk at breakfast and dinner of her seeing her lover during the day, and he his whore. To the humorous astonishment of the audience, when the lover enters in the third scene he turns out to be none other than the husband himself in more rakish attire. The inner psychic conditions of sensuality are met and dramatically conveyed: as financier and wife they are antiseptic with each other, but as lover and whore playing seductive sadomasochistic games, they are able to flaunt them. Their overt relationship is manifestly incongruous and therefore humorous, indicating a challenging ambiguity.

The dramatic action further proceeds on the basis of the couple's inner dynamics and motivations; at the same time, these psychological processes are actually portrayed. A subtle change in the husband takes place after many years of these sporting afternoons. His image of his wife as whore has slowly changed to that of mistress. Because of this new kind of attachment to her, he as husband becomes increasingly jealous of his wife's love for him as lover rather than as husband. In another scene at night, as husband, he for the first time out of jealousy prohibits the continuation of the afternoon love games. But by his very dominance and sadistic manner of prohibition, he once again arouses sexuality in his wife, who then seduces him. Thus, the love-game continues at night as husband and wife, sadist and masochist, seduced and seducer, meet their inner condition of sensuality and find themselves once again as lover and whore.

THE BIRTHDAY PARTY

Here it would be pertinent to take a major, full-length play of Pinter's, *The Birthday Party*, to ascertain how the interrelationship of psyche and social relationship is synthesized and how it differs from *The Homecoming*. Since this is Pinter's earliest major play, it affords an opportunity to see what lines of dramatic development have taken place in his writing.

The plot is a seemingly simple one. Stanley, an emotionally incapacitated concert pianist in his late thirties, lives totally unproductively but securely in a somewhat seedy home of an older couple at a seaside resort. His protectors are a kindly but unexpressive and largely inarticulate man, Mr. Boles, who frequently absents himself to tend his beach chairs; and his motherly wife, Mrs. Boles, a woman unbelievably simpleminded and involved with herself who repeatedly attempts to infantilize and seduce her boarder. Two visitors, "professionals," break menacingly into Stanley's situation of relative security, apparently out to get Stanley for his doublecrossing "the organization." The vagueness of the accusations are reminiscent of Kafka's *The Trial*; in fact, Pinter acknowledges that he has been strongly influenced by Kafka. The older of the visitors, a Jewish man, Goldberg, has an almost unbroken facade of suavity, polish, and good cheer; the other, McCann, an Irishman, is the strong man of the pair. After a birthday party for Stanley in which there is a weirdly ironic mixture of celebration, games, and seduction in an atmosphere of terror and suspense, the men succeed in driving Stanley inarticulately mad and take him away.

Pinter establishes his dramatic approach in this early play by beginning it on a naturalistic note and then changing to increasingly surrealistic action, filled with dread. This Kafkaesque quality enables the play to reach beyond suspenseful melodrama. The evocation of primal fear, the perplexing question of why Stanley should be driven out of his mind, push the viewer to other dimensions of experience and questioning. Again, the critic must allow for multilevel responses to reach an understanding of the play's ambiguity. On one level, there is the metaphor of the violent visitor from whom there is no refuge. On another, there is the certainty of retribution for betrayal of others. On a more psychological level, the play is a picture in depth of a man going insane, describing the very conditions, development, and inner experience of a mental breakdown.

In this last perspective, the viewer must query whether the relationship of Mrs. Boles to Stanley is simply one of landlady to boarder, albeit an odd one. Or if in addition to this obvious fact, the relationship more importantly signifies the simpleminded, narcissistically involved mother who infantilizes and sexually seduces the child for her own ends, as if the child is simply an extension of herself rather than an individual apart. If this be so, then the necessary maternal conditions during childhood for the development of Stanley's breakdown are clearly depicted, aided, and abetted by the relationship with the absentee Mr. Boles, who could possibly have rescued the boy by his presence. Finally, the critic must question whether Goldberg and McCann are characters in their own right only, professionals of an underground organization; or, if seen in this other dimension, they are as well fragments and figments of a paranoid delusion, the messengers of retribution. In this latter view, they would represent malevolent and persecutory creatures of Stanley's own psyche, just as the relationship of Mrs. Boles to Stanley represents an inner picture of the childhood relationship responsible for Stanley's later breakdown.

The setting and theme of childhood are further strikingly evoked through the birthday present of a toy drum from Mrs. Boles to Stanley, then even more through the central dramatic image of the birthday party, where among much merrymaking, they end up playing a child's game of blind-man's buff in an atmosphere of suspense and terror.

Seduction, the harbinger of Stanley's guilt and retribution, becomes highlighted in this scene through variations of Goldberg seducing Lulu, a willing neighbor girl, and of Stanley ending the game of blind-man's buff as the second act ends by trying to rape Lulu, who is found lying spread-eagled on the table, with Stanley giggling over her. Signs of Stanley's impending breakdown are evidenced earlier in the game when his rage emerges toward Mrs. Boles as he tries to strangle her.

The dramatic action in *The Birthday Party* is both shocking and seemingly absurd. But when viewed from the perspective that the characters and their relationships are also projections of a single, tormented psyche (Stanley's) – picturing the conditions, dynamics, and persecutions leading to its breakdown – then the plot becomes a tautly logical presentation on a deep psychic level of reality. On this level, the play is analogous to the dream, where the various characters are all creations or fragments of the single psyche of the dreamer. The tremendous emotional power and enigmatic thrust to *The Birthday Party* thus derives from its paradoxical presentation on both the social and psychic levels of a man being caught up with and destroyed. In this early play Pinter already establishes his use of relatively anonymous characters, an incompleteness of their story, and a seemingly surrealistic plot to allow the viewer's mind to weave back and forth on different levels of experience.

How then does *The Birthday Party* differ from *The Homecoming*, and what dramatic development can be seen? In *The Homecoming* the characters have not only become more developed, but their relationships with each other have also become much better integrated with their own inner psychic states and motivations. A real social situation of a homecoming sets off inner reactions in all of the characters, which determine the characters' interactions. In *The Birthday Party* the social reality of the characters and their relationships are almost more a social facade that masks, while they also simultaneously dramatize the inner reality of a man going insane. In the later play only one character, Ruth, is partially a non-character used to convey the internalized images of others. The other characters portray their own internalized image-relationships through dramatic action: e.g., Teddy having eaten Lenny's sandwich; Max at the end groveling for Ruth's love as she pats Joey's head. This contrasts with *The Birthday Party*, where all of the characters, with the exception of Stanley, are partially non-characters portraying Stanley's state of mind.

Thus, Pinter is able to achieve a much more complex interrelationship between character interaction and inner psychic images in *The Homecoming*. *The Lover* then may be viewed as an intermediary piece, where Pinter is able to achieve the simultaneous portrayal of psychic and social reality between two characters – at once more complex than the single psyche of *The Birthday Party*, but not nearly the achievement of *The Homecoming*. Finally, the visitor, while having equally profound effects in *The Homecoming*, enters the play in a more naturalistic way and is far less obviously malevolent than in *The Birthday Party*.

Reflections: an Afterword

As I reflect on this work and a previous book, *In Search of Self in India and Japan: Toward a Cross-Cultural Psychology* (Roland, 1988), two things stand out. In both works, I have made a serious effort for an interdisciplinary integration, rather than simply treading the well-worn path of applied psychoanalysis that more often than not is pervaded by reductionistic assumptions. In *Dreams and Drama*, I attempt to integrate psychoanalysis with art and the artist. In *In Search of Self*, I interrelated clinical psychoanalytic data of Indians and Japanese with culture, social organization, and social change. Although published before *Dreams and Drama*, *In Search of Self* greatly benefited from interdisciplinary aspirations of some of the chapters in this current book, which were originally written still earlier.

Even more important, in both books, I view psychoanalysis and the psychological as paradoxically both standing on their own and as being encompassed by the other discipline. In *Dreams and Drama*, the primary process in the arts and in the artist is used and governed by the imaginative part of the secondary process that expresses an artistic vision through poetic metaphor, paradox, and various formal elements. Whereas in *In Search of Self*, the psychological makeup of persons is structured and governed by civilizational principles that encompass overarching cultural factors, sociocultural patterns, and sociohistorical change.

Parts II and III of this book, "Dreams, imagery, and creativity" and "Psychoanalytic criticism," are oriented around two basic insights, one coming from a dream, the other from one of my etchings. The first is that the primary process in dreams can only express incipient paradoxes and incomplete poetic metaphors, in contrast to art which clearly relies on both paradox and poetic metaphor. Artistic vision and meanings then clearly relate to an imaginative part of the secondary process, as distinct from the more usual logical, rational, and casual thinking.

The second insight is that imagery bypasses defense, which means that the artist's use of imagery can simultaneously convey poetic metaphor and paradox on the one hand, and metaphorically, unconscious fantasies and affect from the primary process on the other. The latter emotionally fuels the artistic meanings. These insights are in the context of a broadening view of both the primary process (Noy, 1969; Deri, 1984) and the secondary process (Rothenberg, 1979).

I have used these basic insights as a platform in Part III for critiquing both the contributions and the pervasive reductionism in so much psychoanalytic criticism and notions of artistic creativity. And it is just these insights that give a grounding for serious efforts in psychoanalytic drama criticism in the last two chapters on Pirandello's and Pinter's plays. Here, the endeavor is to integrate drama criticism involving the artistic vision and meanings of these plays involving their central metaphors, paradoxes, and formal elements with the emotional power of primary-process symbolization. These chapters on Pirandello and Pinter thus follow in an integral way my earlier perspective.

Part I, "The artist and the artistic process," was written much more recently. It needed many more years of experience of both working with a number of artist patients, including the career artists in Chapter 1, and of my own experience as a visual artist and dramatist. Here, I am departing from Winnicott's theories of creativity and the self as applicable to everyone to carve out the specifics of fashioning an artist self, artistic creativity, and the struggles that career artists undergo.

As with any work, there are significant omissions. The turn in psychoanalytic criticism in the last two plus decades has shifted considerably toward Lacanian-influenced and other French theory. This is obviously a highly complex subject in and of itself; one I am not sufficiently steeped in to write about meaningfully. Although I collaborated in the first invitation of Lacanian and other French psychoanalysts to come to the United States to present their work at a major conference in 1976,[1] and then hosted bimonthly meetings of French analysts with my New York City colleagues for several years, it became obvious that I would need a much more thorough immersion in French psychoanalysis to understand it in depth. As I mentioned in the Introduction, I must leave such discussions for Lacanian psychoanalysts-artists.

Nevertheless, even with this omission in the area of psychoanalytic criticism, I believe there is much in this book that contributes importantly to the dialogue between psychoanalysis and the arts and the artist.

NOTES

1.   Serge Doubrovsky of the French Department of New York University and I organized the conference, "Culture and Self: A French and American Dialogue." I later edited and contributed to the book of the conference papers, *Psychoanalysis, Creativity, and Literature: A French and American Dialogue*, Columbia University Press, 1978.

References

Aaron, S. 1986. *Stage Fright: its Role in Acting.* Chicago: University of Chicago Press.

Alexander, F. 1963. "The psychoanalyst looks at contemporary art." In *Art and Psychoanalysis,* ed. W. Phillips. Cleveland: World Publishing.

Altman, L. 1969. *The Dream in Psychoanalysis.* New York: International Universities Press.

Angyal, A. 1965. *Neurosis and Treatment: a Holistic Theory.* New York: Wiley.

Arieti, S. 1967. *The Intrapsychic Self.* New York: Basic Books.

Arlow, J. A. and C. Brenner. 1964. "Dreams and the structural theory." In *Psychoanalytic Concepts and the Structural Theory.* New York: International Universities Press.

Bacal, H. and K. Newman 1990. *Theories of Object Relations: Bridges to Self Psychology (Personality, Psychopathology, and Psychotherapy).* New York: Columbia University Press.

Bentley, E. 1966. "Il tragico imperatore." *Tulane Drama Review,* 10:60–75.

—— 1968. "Father's day." *Tulane Drama Review,* 13:57–72.

Bergmann, M. S. 1966. "The intrapsychic and communicative aspects of the dream." *International Journal Psycho-Analysis.* 47:356–63.

Bollas, C. 1987. *The Shadow of the Object: Psychoanalysis of the Unthought Known.* New York: Columbia University Press.

Brenman-Gibson, M. 1981. *Clifford Odets: American Playwright.* New York: Atheneum.

Brooks, C. 1960. "The language of paradox." In *The Language of Poetry,* ed. A. Tate. New York: Russell & Russell.

Brown, R. 1958. *Words and Things.* Glencoe, IL: Free Press.

Burke, K. 1941a. *The Philosophy of Literary Form.* New York: Random House, 1957.

―― 1941b. "Freud and the analysis of poetry." In *The Philosophy of Literary Form*. Baton Rouge: Louisiana State University Press.

―― 1953. "Psychology and form." In *Counterstatement*. Berkeley and Los Angeles: University of California Press.

Bush, M. 1967. "The problem of form in the psychoanalytic theory of art." *Psychoanalytic Review*, 54:5–35.

Chasseguet-Smirgal, J. 1984. *Creativity and Perversion*. New York: W. W. Norton.

Coltart, N. 1992. "The practice of psychoanalysis and Buddhism." In *Slouching toward Bethlehem*. New York: Guilford Press, pp. 164–75.

―― 1996. "Buddhism and psychoanalysis revisited." In *The Baby and the Bathwater*. New York: International Universities Press, pp. 125–40.

Cooper, P. 1998. "The disavowal of the spirit: integration and wholeness in Buddhism and Psychoanalysis." In *The Couch and the Tree: Dialogues in Psychoanalysis and Buddhism*, ed. A. Molino. New York: North Point Press, pp. 231–46.

―― 1999. "Buddhist meditation and countertransference: a case study." *American Journal Psychoanalysis*, 59:71–86.

Crews, F. 1976. *Out of My System*. New York: Oxford University Press.

Davis, R. G. 1963. "Art and anxiety." In *Art and Psychoanalysis*, ed. W. Phillips. Cleveland: World Publishing.

Deri, S. 1984. *Symbolization and Creativity*. New York: International Universities Press.

Doubrovsky, S. 1978. " 'The nine of hearts': fragment of a psycho-reading of *La Nausée*." In *Psychoanalysis, Creativity, and Literature: a French–American Dialogue*, ed. A. Roland. New York: Columbia University Press.

Dukore, B. F. 1971. "A woman's place." In *A Casebook on Harold Pinter's The Homecoming*, ed. J. Lahr. New York: Grove Press.

Dumont, L. 1986. *Essays in Individualism*. Chicago: University of Chicago Press.

Edel, L. 1953. *Henry James*. New York: Lippincott.

―― 1969. "Hawthorne's symbolism and psychoanalysis." In *Hidden Patterns: Studies in Psychoanalytic Literary Criticism*, ed. Leonard and Eleanor Manheim. New York: Macmillan.

Ehrenzweig, A. 1953. *The Psychoanalysis of Artistic Vision and Hearing*. New York: George Braziller.

—— 1967. *The Hidden Order of Art*. Berkeley, CA: University of California Press.

Eigen, M. 1996. *The Psychoanalytic Mystic*. Binghamton, NY: ESF.

Eissler, K. 1971. Discourse on Hamlet and "Hamlet". New York: International Universities Press.

Empson, W. 1930. *Seven Types of Ambiguity*. New York: New Directions, 1947.

—— 1963. "*Alice in Wonderland:* the child as swain." In *Art and Psychoanalysis,* ed. W. Phillips. Cleveland: World Publishing.

Erikson, E. H. 1950. *Childhood and Society*. New York: Norton.

—— 1954. "The dream specimen of psychoanalysis." *Journal American Psychoanalytic Association*, 2:5–56.

—— 1968. *Identity, Youth, and Crisis*. New York: W. W. Norton.

—— 1969. *Gandhi's Truth*. New York: W. W. Norton

Esslin, M. 1961. *The Theatre of the Absurd*. Garden City, NY: Doubleday.

—— 1971. "*The Homecoming:* an interpretation." In *A Casebook on Harold Pinter's The Homecoming*, ed. J. Lahr. New York: Grove Press.

Fairbairn, R. 1952. *Psychoanalytic Studies of the Personality*. London: Tavistock Publishers.

Federn, P. 1952. *Ego Psychology and the Psychoses*. New York: Basic Books.

Feirstein, F. 1991. "Psychoanalysis and creativity." In *Poetry after Modernism,* ed. Robert McDowell. Ashland, OR: Storyline Press.

—— 1997. "Psychoanalysis and poetry." *Partisan Review*, summer, pp. 433–9.

Ferenczi S. 1913. "To whom does one relate one's dreams?" In *Further Contributions to the Theory and Technique of Psychoanalysis*. London: Hogarth Press, 1950.

Fiedler, L. A. 1963. "Archetype and signature." In *Art and Psycho-analysis*, ed. W. Phillips. Cleveland: World Publishing.

Fosshagen, J. L. 1987. *Dream Interpretation: A Comparative Study*, rev. ed. New York: PMA Publications.

French, T. and E. Fromm. 1964. *Dream Interpretation*. New York: Basic Books.

Freud, S. 1900. "The interpretation of dreams." *Standard Edition*, 4–5. London: Hogarth Press.

—— 1907. "Delusion and dreams in Jensen's Gradiva." *Standard Edition*, 9. London: Hogarth Press.

—— 1908. "The relationship of the poet to daydreaming." *Standard Edition*, 9. London: Hogarth Press.

—— 1915. "Some psychopathological characters on the stage." *Psychoanalytic Quarterly,* 11, 1942.

—— 1923a. "Remarks upon the theory and practice of dream interpretation." *Standard Edition*, 19. London: Hogarth Press.

—— 1923b. "The ego and the id." *Standard Edition*, 19. London: Hogarth Press.

Frye, N. 1957. *Anatomy of Criticism*. Princeton: Princeton University Press.

Gilligan, C. 1980. *In a Different Voice*. Cambridge: Harvard University Press.

Gombrich, E. H. 1957. "Psychoanalysis and the history of art." In *Freud and the Twentieth Century*. New York: Meridian Books.

Greenson, R. R. 1970. "The exceptional position of the dream in psychoanalytic practice." *Psychoanalytic Quarterly*. 39:519–49.

Grinker, R. 1957. "On identification." *International Journal Psycho-Analysis,* 38:379–90.

Hagman, G. 2000. "The creative process." In *Progress in Self Psychology*, ed. A. Goldberg, 16:277–97.

Hall, P. 1971. "A director's approach: an interview with Peter Hall." In *A Casebook on Harold Pinter's The Homecoming*, ed. J. Lahr. New York: Grove Press.

Hardwick, E. 1967. "Review of Pinter's *The Homecoming*." *New York Review*, February 23, p. 10.

Hartmann, H. 1964. *Essays on Ego Psychology*. New York: International Universities Press.

Hendrick, I. 1942. "Instinct and the ego during infancy." *Psychoanalytic Quarterly,* 11:33–58.

Hewes, H. 1967. "Interview with Pinter." *Saturday Review*, April 8.

Hoffman, F. 1957. *Freudianism and the Literary Mind*. Baton Rouge: Louisiana State University Press.

Holland, N. 1964. *Psychoanalysis and Shakespeare*. New York: McGraw Hill.

—— 1968. *The Dynamics of Literary Response*. New York: Oxford University Press.

—— 1973. *Poems in Person: an Introduction to the Psychoanalysis of Literature*. New York: Oxford University Press.

—— 1975. *5 Readers Reading*. New Haven, CT: Yale University Press.

Hyman, S. E. 1948. "Maud Bodkin and psychological criticism." In *The Armed Vision*. New York: Knopf.

Jacobs, T. 1974. "Discussion of Martin Wangh's paper on Pirandello." Presented at the New York Psychoanalytic Institute, January, 1974.

Jacobson, E. 1964. *The Self and the Object World*. New York: International Universities Press.

Jones, E. 1916. "The theory of symbolism." In *Papers on Psychoanalysis*, 2nd edn. London: Bailliere, Tindall & Cox, 1918.

—— 1948. "The death of Hamlet's father." *International Journal Psycho-Analysis*, 29:174–6.

Kainer, R. 1990. "The precursor as mentor, the therapist as muse: creativity and selfobject phenomena." In *Progress in Self Psychology*, ed. A. Goldberg, 6:175–88.

Kanzer, M. 1955. "The communicative function of the dream." *International Journal Psycho-Analysis*, 36:260–266.

Kernberg, O. 1975. *Borderline Conditions and Pathological Narcissism*. New York: Jason Aronson.

Klauber, J. 1967. "On the significance of reporting dreams in psychoanalysis." *International Journal Psycho-Analysis*, 48:424–32.

Klein, G. 1976. *Psychoanalytic Theory: an Exploration of Essentials*. New York: International Universities Press.

Klein, M. 1930. "The importance of symbol-formation in the development of the ego." In *Contributions to Psychoanalysis*. London: Hogarth Press, 1948.

Kligerman, C. 1962. "A psychoanalytic study of *Six Characters in Search of an Author.*" *Journal American Psychoanalytic Association*, 10:731–4.

Kohut, H. 1971. *Analysis of the Self*. New York: International Universities Press.

—— 1977. *Restoration of the Self*. New York: International Universities Press.

—— 1984. *How Does Analysis Cure?* Chicago: University of Chicago Press.

Kott, J. 1964. *Shakespeare Our Contemporary*. New York: Doubleday.

Kris, E. 1952. *Psychoanalytic Explorations on Art*. New York: International Universities Press.

Kubie, L. S. 1958. *Neurotic Distortions of the Creative Process*. New York: Noonday Press.

—— 1978. *Symbol and Neurosis. Psychological Issues, Monograph 44*. New York: International Universities Press.

Lahr, J. 1971. "Pinter's language." In *A Casebook on Harold Pinter's The Homecoming,* ed. John Lahr. New York: Grove Press.

Laing, R. 1965. *The Divided Self.* Baltimore: Penguin Books.

Langer, S. 1942. *Philosophy in a New Key.* New York: Penguin Books.

—— 1953. *Feeling and Form.* New York: Scribner.

—— 1957. *Problems of Art.* New York: Charles Scribner's Sons.

Lazarre, J. 1978. "The mother-artist: woman as trickster." In *Career and Motherhood: Struggles for a New Identity*, ed. A. Roland and B. Harris. New York: Human Sciences Press.

Lesser, S. O. 1957. *Fiction and the Unconscious.* Boston: Beacon Press.

Lichtenstein, H. 1977. *The Dilemma of Human Identity.* New York: Jason Aronson.

Long, R. W. 2001. "Modernism, Judaism, and issues of identity: the photography of Lucia Moholy." Presented at Congress of World Union of Jewish Studies, Jerusalem, August, 2001.

Lynd, H. 1958. *On Shame and the Search for Identity.* New York: Science Editions.

Mahler, M. 1968. *On Human Symbiosis and the Vicissitudes of Individuation.* New York: International Universities Press.

Mahler, M., F. Pine, and A. Bergman. 1975. *Psychological Birth of the Human Infant.* New York: Basic Books.

McDougall, J. 1991. *Theaters of the Mind.* New York: Brunner-Maisel.

Menaker, E. 1953. "Masochism: a defense reaction of the ego." *Psychoanalytic Quarterly.* 27:205–20.

—— 1982. *Otto Rank: a Rediscovered Legacy.* New York: Columbia University Press.

Menaker, E. and W. Menaker. 1965. *Ego in Evolution.* New York: Grove Press.

Milner, M. 1952. "The role of illusion in symbol formation." In *New Directions in Psychoanalysis*, ed. M. Klein *et al.* New York: Basic Books.

—— 1957. *On not Being Able to Paint.* New York: International Universities Press.

—— 1987. *The Suppressed Madness of Sane Men.* London: Tavistock.

Morris, K. 1966. "*The Homecoming.*" *Tulane Drama Review*, winter, pp. 185–91.

Nelson, B. 1968. "Avant-garde dramatists from Ibsen to Ionesco." *Psychoanalytic Review*, 55:505–12.

Noy, P. 1968. "A theory of art and aesthetic experience." *Psychoanalytic Review*, 55:623–45.

—— 1969. "A revision of the psychoanalytic theory of the primary process." *International Journal Psychoanal.* 50:155–78.

—— 1979. "Form creation in art: an ego psychological approach to creativity." *Psychoanalytic Quarterly*, 48:229–56.

Nuetzel, E. 1995. "Unconscious phenomena in the process of theater: preliminary hypotheses." *Psychoanalytic Quarterly*, 64:345–52.

—— 1999a. "Acting and enacting: a case study in the evolution of theatrical performance." *Journal of Applied Psychoanalysis*, 1:79–101.

—— 1999b. "Psychoanalysis as a dramatic art." *Annual of Psychoanalysis*, 26–27: 295–313.

—— 2000. "Psychoanalysis and dramatic art." *Journal of Applied Psychoanalytic Studies*, 2:41–63.

Ornstein, P. H. 1987. "On self-state dreams in the psychoanalytic treatment process." In *The Interpretation of Dreams in Clinical Work*, ed. A. Rothstein. New York: Internation Universities Press, pp. 87–104.

Overby, A. and H. Freudenberger. 1969. "Patients from an emotionally deprived environment." *Psychoanalytic Review*, 56:299–312.

Piaget, J. 1962. *Play, Dreams, and Imitation in Childhood*. New York: Grove Press.

Pinter, H. 1967. Interview. *New Yorker*, February 25.

Pirandello, L. 1952. *Six Characters in Search of an Author* and *Henry IV*. In *Naked Masks: Five plays by Luigi Pirandello*, ed. E. Bentley. New York: Dutton.

Rank, O. 1932. *Art and the Artist*. New York: Knopf.

Rank, O. and H. Sachs. 1913. *The Significance of Psychoanalysis for the Mental Sciences. Monograph 23*. New York: Nervous and Mental Diseases Publishing Company, 1915.

Rappaport, D. 1951. *Organization and Pathology of Thought*. New York: Columbia University Press.

Riviere, J. 1957. "The inner world in Ibsen's *The Master-Builder*." In *New Directions in Psychoanalysis*, ed. M. Klein, P. Heimann, and R. E. Mony-Kyrle. New York: Basic Books.

Roheim, G. 1963. "Myth and folk tale." In *Art and Psychoanalysis*, ed. W. Phillips. Cleveland: World Publishing.

Roland, A. 1988. *In Search of Self in India and Japan: Toward a Cross-cultural Psychology*. Princeton: Princeton University Press.

—— 1996. *Cultural Pluralism and Psychoanalysis: The Asian and North American Experience*. New York and London: Routledge.

—— 1999. "The spiritual self and psychopathology: theoretical reflections and clinical observations." *Psychoanalysis and Psychotherapy,* 16:211–34.

Rose, G. 1980. *The Power of Form: a Psychoanalytic Approach to Aesthetic Form.* Madison, CT: International Universities Press.

Rotenberg, C. 1988. "Selfobject theory and the artistic process." In *Progress in Self Psychology,* ed. A. Goldberg, 4:193–213.

Rothenberg, A. 1969. "The iceman changeth: toward an empirical approach to creativity." *Journal American Psychoanal. Assoc.* 17:549–607.

—— 1973. "The defense of psychoanalysis in literature." *Comparative Drama,* 7:51–67.

—— 1976. "Homospatial thinking in creativity." *Archives General Psychiatry,* 29.

—— 1979. *Creativity: the Emerging Goddess.* Chicago: University of Chicago Press.

Rubin, J. 1996. *Psychotherapy and Buddhism: Toward an Integration.* New York: Plenum Press.

Rycroft, C. 1968. *Imagination and Reality.* New York: International Universities Press.

—— 1975. "Freud and the imagination." *New York Review,* 22.

Sachs, H. 1942. *The Creative Unconscious.* Cambridge: Sci-Art Publishing.

Schachtel, E. 1961. "On alienated concepts of identity." *American Journal of Psychoanalysis,* 21:120–31.

Schafer, R. 1968. *Aspects of Internalization.* New York: International Universities Press.

Schechner, R. 1966. "Puzzling Pinter." *Tulane Drama Review,* winter, pp. 176–84.

Schilder, P. 1953. *Medical Psychology.* New York: International Universities Press.

Searles, R. 1966. "Concerning the development of an identity." *Psychoanalytic Review,* 53:5–7–530.

Segal, H. 1957. "A psychoanalytic approach to aesthetics." In *New Directions in Psychoanalysis,* ed. M. Klein, P. Heimann, and R. E. Mony-Kyrle. New York: Basic Books.

Sharpe, E. F. 1937. *Dream Analysis.* London: Hogarth Press, 1961.

Sheppard, E. and L. J. Saul. 1958. "An approach to a systematic study of ego function." *Psychoanalytic Quarterly,* 27:237–45.

Spitz, R. A. 1965. *The First Year of Life.* New York: International Universities Press.

Sullivan, H. S. 1953. *The Interpersonal Theory of Psychiatry*. New York: W. W. Norton.

Tomkins, S. 1947. *The Thematic Apperception Test: The Theory and Technique of Interpretation*. New York: Grune & Stratton.

Trilling, L. 1963. "Art and neurosis." In *Art and Psychoanalysis*, ed. W. Phillips. Cleveland: World Publishing.

Waldhorn, H. F. (ed.) 1967. *The Place of the Dream in Clinical Psychoanalysis. Kris Study Group, Monograph* 2. New York: International Universities Press.

Walker, A. 1971. "Why the lady does it." In *A Casebook on Harold Pinter's The Homecoming*, ed. J. Lahr. New York: Grove Press.

Wangh, M. 1976. "Underlying motivations in Pirandello's *Six Characters in Search of an Author.*" *Journal American Psychoanalytic Association*, 24.

Weber, M. 1920. "Introduction." In *The Protestant Ethic and the Spirit of Capitalism*. New York: Scribner.

Weil, E. 1958. "The origins and vicissitudes of the self-image." *Psychoanalytic Review*, 45: 3–19.

Weiss, E. 1960. *The Structure and Dynamics of the Human Mind*. New York: International Universities Press.

Weissman, P. 1965. *Creativity in the Theatre*. New York: Dell.

Werner, H. 1948. *Comparative Psychology of Mental Development*. New York: International Universities Press.

White, R. 1964. "Ego and reality in psychoanalytic theory." *Psychological Issues,* 3.

Winnicott, D. W. 1958. "Psychoanalysis and the sense of guilt." In *The Maturational Processes and the Facilitating Environment*, 15–36, 1965. New York: International Universities Press.

—— 1965. *The Maturational Processes and the Facilitating Environment*. New York: International Universities Press.

Index